OUTSIDE THE NUTSHELL

John Coyle

authorHOUSE

AuthorHouse™ UK Ltd.
500 Avebury Boulevard
Central Milton Keynes, MK9 2BE
www.authorhouse.co.uk
Phone: 08001974150

OUTSIDE THE NUTSHELL

Content copyright © John Coyle, 2010.
Illustrations copyright © Kevin Coyle 2010.

All rights reserved. No portion of this book may be reproduced, stored in a retrieval system or transmitted at any time or by any means mechanical, electronic, photocopying, recording or otherwise, without prior, written permission of the author.

The right of John Coyle to be identified as the author of this work has been asserted by him in accordance with Copyright, Design and Patents act 1988

All third-party trademarks are hereby acknowledged.

For more information and contact details see

http://www.outsidethenutshell.co.uk/

ISBN: 9781452044712
First Published by Author House: 2/18/2011

Any people depicted in stock imagery provided by Thinkstock are models, and such images are being used for illustrative purposes only. Certain stock imagery © Thinkstock.

This book is printed on acid-free paper.

Because of the dynamic nature of the Internet, any Web addresses or links contained in this book may have changed since publication and may no longer be valid. The views expressed in this work are solely those of the author and do not necessarily reflect the views of the publisher, and the publisher hereby disclaims any responsibility for them.

Outside the Nutshell

Have you ever thought why things so rarely seem to go to plan? Do you find success elusive? Do you find positive outcomes outweighed by negative issues? Or are you starting something new and are nervous of the challenge?

This book aims to help you by looking at what is success and what is not. It looks at how to survive and how to succeed. You may be aware of all of this but please read with an open mind....

I have titled the book "Outside the Nutshell" as there are numerous books that try to convey something in a Nutshell (there are 1,290 Nutshell titles on Amazon to date including Grape Growing and Quantum Theory) but to be successful we need to know more than the succinct guide or summary. I have tried to present what I think makes the difference between completing the task (following the Nutshell guide) and being successful in the engagement (stepping Outside the Nutshell).

In times past, a son learnt his trade from his father, he would spend countless hours watching and learning and eventually copying in the field, the forge, as a steward, in the workshop etc. I accept that not all people should follow their parent's career (and I have not done so) and it should certainly not be the only option available to them but we now seem to expect people to pick up a lot of skills and abilities via text books or a brief handover.

I hope from this book that you might learn something of value to you from my experiences. But your experiences are as valid as mine. So by me initiating and sharing my experience and then prompting you to add your own you can decide how all this together can help you get more Outside the Nutshell. If you can go through this book with other people and share your experiences together then even better.

I do not claim that this book is either unique or that the content is not already widely known. And I do not claim to be perfect. Consequently a lot of the ideals have not always been achieved -

Success versus Completion – Your Choice

actually a lot of the experiences have stemmed from a failure to meet ideals or being on the brink of failure, but we learn a lot from our mistakes and we also learn when we appreciate that we have avoided mistakes.

How to Use this Book

You can use this book in any way that you want! Some suggested options are:-

- To read it
- To use it as part of a development programme with your colleagues / associates
- To read it and complete the exercises
- To carry it with you for reference

If you do decide to complete the exercises I would encourage you to do the following.

> *Take time over each exercise: think, assess, step back and re-visit. There are no better or best answers, it is what benefits you and your circumstances that matters.*

Please feel free to read the whole book before tackling the exercises (you do not have to) but please also tackle each exercise separately and take time over it.

Thank You

John Coyle

CONTENTS

Outside the Nutshell I
How to Use this Book II

SECTION 1   INTRODUCTION 1

Towards Success 3
Success versus Completion 5
A Pause for Perspective 7
Where do we go from here? 13

SECTION 2   KEY PRINCIPLES 15

Identify Your Values 17
Think 21
Get a Balance 23
Know Your Skills 27
Growth 29
Key Principles recap 31

SECTION 3   APPLICATION 33

Overview 35
Pre-assignment 37
Start-Up 45
Initiation to Stability 55
Stability and Building on it 63
Finishing 69
Success and Failure 73
Templates and Guides 81

SECTION 4   CONCLUSION AND WRAP UP 91

Review 93

SECTION 5   PERSONAL FOCUS/EXERCISES 99

INDEX 139

Success versus Completion – Your Choice

Section 1
Introduction

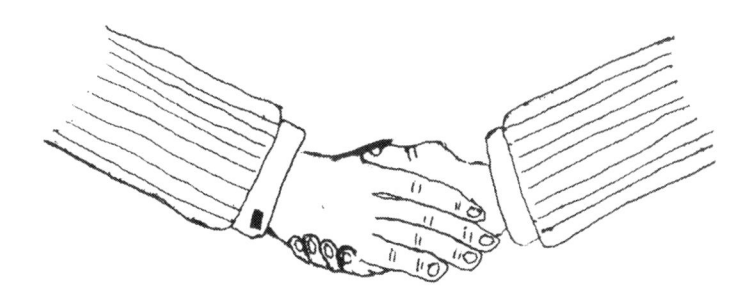

Introduction

Success versus Completion – Your Choice

Introduction

Towards Success

Via a combination of personal experiences (anecdotal, practical, humorous and serious), existing practices and participation, my objectives are to

- Make us step back and think
- Learn from our experiences because we step back and think
- Learn from others' experiences because they have stepped back and thought
- Engage people and build teamwork
- Identify how and where we can achieve success, where it benefits most and what it looks like - or what the lack of it looks like
- Move people from a completion and employment attitude and encourage a success and engagement attitude

Namely
To provide a benefit that matters and is not outweighed by negative results

Experience makes us think we know how to manage ourselves and our work – but do we? If it was blindingly obvious (or even just marginally visible) why are so many projects over budget by £xxxx and overrun by xxx months / years – so often??!!

I hope the outcome will enable people and businesses to be better equipped to deal with, understand and work with delivery focused teams and individuals both within and outside our organisations. I hope they will have a better understanding of peoples' behaviours and I hope they will be re-energised and refreshed by periodically stepping back, thinking and assessing. The result will hopefully enable us all to work more effectively and successfully in delivering (both internally and externally) on time, to quality and to budget **together**!

I also hope it will increase opportunities for re-engagements, improve motivation throughout the business and increase revenue.

I want to encourage success by giving some guidelines and assistance. Unfortunately this is not formulaic, if you take everything you read here and apply it as stated you could still FAIL!! I explain why later but the reason is rooted in the logic for Outside the Nutshell. If you accept that most of learning is done on the job then Training and Coaching (and reading this book) supplement Practice and Experience, but are no match or substitute for it.

Success versus Completion

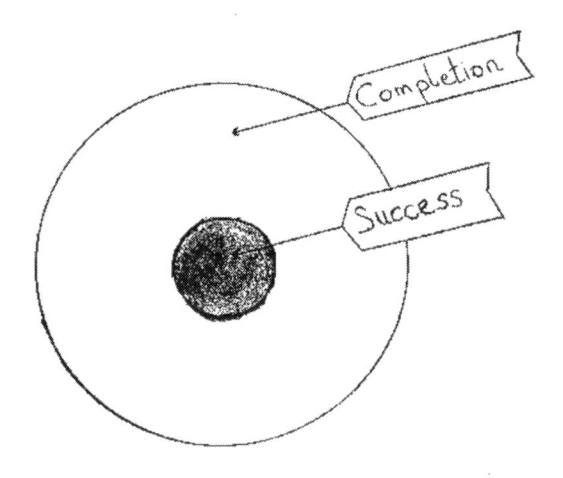

There is an old joke about a man walking along a country road and seeing two workers. One is digging holes and the other is following behind filling them in. The man asks the first worker what he is doing and is told that there are normally 3 of them - he digs the holes, Joe inserts the telegraph poles and Fred fills in the holes. Although Joe is off sick today no-one can complain about them slacking on the job or making excuses as they are working just as they normally do.

This is a joke but the following actually happened to me…

I was in Liverpool St. Station in London waiting for a train. As the departure time approached, the train details were on the indicator board but no platform was displayed. Just as the departure time approached the platform number appeared so I very briskly made my way to the indicated platform only to find the train already heading out of the station, empty! I complained to one of the staff and was told that the train arrived in the station as 6 carriages but they had to split it into 2 trains of 3 carriages and for health and safety reasons they are not allowed to announce the platform until this is completed. Unfortunately this was not completed until the departure time was imminent. Their service level is measured on the trains leaving in a timely manner so they uncoupled the train, announced the platform and then the train left before any passengers could get to it. I was angry at the time but on reflection afterwards I realised that not only was this behaviour ridiculous but that the train actually met its Customer Success Criteria (i.e. on time) so it will have been entered in the month end statistics as a success.

In both cases, one surreal but the other true, the people involved, quite clearly, completed their tasks but did not actually achieve **success.**

What I would like to do is to explore what the difference between **completion** and **success** is and identify some ways of "bridging the gap". I believe we encounter and encourage the **completion** mentality much more often than is necessary and I also believe we can take steps to bridge that gap to achieve a greater level of **success**. Ultimately, this is in the interest of everyone.

Introduction

A Pause for Perspective

I would like to present 3 analogies. Please bear in mind that they are only analogies so they inevitably breakdown at some stage. However, I would like to use them to emphasise my point and to try to illustrate what I am trying to achieve. I will explain more at the end of this section. I would like to use a Family Wedding, Climbing Everest and an Outward Bound Team Building event.

Obviously not all Weddings, scalings of Everest or Outward Bound events will be like the following so please bear that in mind!

Φ A Family Wedding

What is/are the objective(s)?...If you are a guest then you want to share in the celebration of a friend or relation, you want a good, well run event but not necessarily at the expense of other things. If you are the bride or groom you want others to celebrate with you.

"Remind me, why are we here?"

If you are the bride or groom and are having a church service and you have a relation who is a minister then you might well want them to lead the service. You would probably not ask them to sit in the congregation on the basis that you had found someone who is better at leading the service!

You do not say to the best man or groom "Look, Uncle Jim is better at making speeches, has more experience, holds the audience better and is much wittier than you. You skip the speeches and leave them to him".

Success versus Completion – Your Choice

If you are a guest, you want to encourage the bride and groom, comment on how well they have done and support them in the bits they might find difficult (e.g. first waltz, speeches). You are supportive and positive and you go the extra mile to make the event special.

Afterwards people will ask "How was the wedding?" It is an open, subjective question, soliciting your opinion, but "Did you enjoy it?" will figure prominently.

Φ Climbing Everest

This is a single objective event - to get to the top. You only go with people who have the same objective and who are dedicated and evidently capable and experienced. Everything you do both individually and together is focused on securing that objective.

You spend months, if not years, planning it and you spend a lot of time with your fellow climbers planning, training and identifying the right equipment, techniques, routes and roles.

You also assess - and not just subconsciously - the others to see if there are any weaknesses that may hold you all back and, if so, you work to address them.

You would most probably not bring along sightseers, family members for the sake of it or people who want to absorb the local cultures or study the wildlife.

Once you have started, any setbacks or hitches are addressed in a way that enables you to reach the top. If someone gets hurt you leave them behind in the care of a backup team. You have hopefully thought of each possible eventuality in advance and have a plan in place to deal with it.

It is a single objective and success depends on whether it is achieved or not. People will just ask "Did you make it to the top?" This is much more specific and much less subjective than the wedding!

Φ An Outward Bound Team Building event

This is the kind of event that you might sign up for with total strangers but is usually done with colleagues or a social club to enhance team relationships, have some fun and get to know each other better.

What you have is a mixture of individuals with some objective being set. For the sake of this analogy let's say you are all being dropped off at an unknown location in the morning with a pile of equipment and an objective is to find your way to a named location by sunset.

It seems clear what you want to achieve but different people will have different perspectives and propose different ways of accomplishing the objective. The rules will not always be that clear. People will start asking

> *"Do we have to stay together or does only one of us have to reach the location?"*
> *"Do we go at the speed of the slowest, fastest or average?"*
> *"What equipment do we need to take and what can we leave?"*
> *"Who knows about outdoor survival and how much do we trust them?"*
> *"Is keeping relationships more important than meeting the objectives or vice versa?"*

As you progress, it becomes apparent that people have made assumptions that others do not agree with or are not aware of. For example, if someone gets hurt do you call for help and abandon the objective (Compassion and Mercy) or do you push on and carry them (Success and Determination)? Neither is right nor wrong but is based on an individual's characteristics and interpretation of instructions.

To add to the confusion, individuals may have specific objectives for medical care, equipment care, keeping the team together etc.

If someone asks afterwards "How was the teambuilding event?" this could be answered in any number of ways, depending on who is asked. Success or failure is harder to define and may only materialise long after the event. Meeting the objectives (i.e. getting to the destination) is clearly not the sole criterion for success. In some cases, it could be largely irrelevant to the overall success!

Φ So What's the Point?

At work, we may have one or several objectives, it would be nice to think that that was all we had to concern ourselves with (our Everest) but...

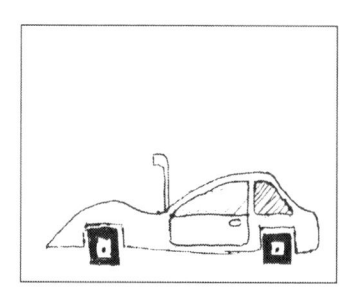

...the Outward Bound event, although it is messier than the others, is more like real life and work. Different people have different objectives, sometimes pulling in opposite directions, even though the overall goal may seem to be the same.

We might have a clear objective (our Everest) but those around us may not - or their "Everest" may be different from ours. We may also have to create or at least clarify our own objectives.

We have to work with those around us to achieve success and not just deliver a completed task (although usually a "completed task" is important, if not essential).

If we meet our objectives but nobody else around us meets theirs (or nobody will work with us again) then we have completed the task but **not** been successful. If everybody else met their objectives

Success versus Completion – Your Choice

and will work with us again but we did not meet our objectives then we have **neither** completed the task **nor** been successful.

This means that at times we need to be focused and achievement centred and at other times we need to be supportive and encouraging. Much of the time we need a combination.

What I would like to look at next is how we can complete the task *and* have a successful engagement.

Success versus Completion – Your Choice

Where do we go from here?

Orientation... I would like to cover the following, in my opinion they are essential to encouraging success

Theory - Establish *5 Key Principles*.

- *1* - Identify your VALUES
- *2* - THINK
- *3* - Get a BALANCE
- *4* – Know Your SKILLS
- *5* – GROW (we can improve)

Application - Applying the *5 Key Principles* above to address the following areas

- Pre-assignment
- Start up / Initiation / Arrival at a New Job, Project or Assignment
- Initiation to Stability (the first few weeks or months)
- Stability and Building on it
- Finishing, Signing Off and Getting Out
- Success and Failure throughout the cycle

Conclusion – Identify learning, review and apply

Success versus Completion – Your Choice

Section 2
Key Principles

Principle's office 1

Principle's office 2

Principle's office 3

Principle's office 4

Principle's office 5

(Choices)

Success versus Completion – Your Choice

Success versus Completion – Your Choice

Values   Page 17

Identify Your Values

The Dictionary definition of Values may be something like

> *The beliefs people have about what is
> right, wrong or most important in their life
> which influence their behaviour*

A change in categories used by my employer in its Performance Review and Assessment process forced me to sit down with the old and new areas. I tried to map them so I could understand what behaviours in the old system matched behaviours in the new system. I got the following…

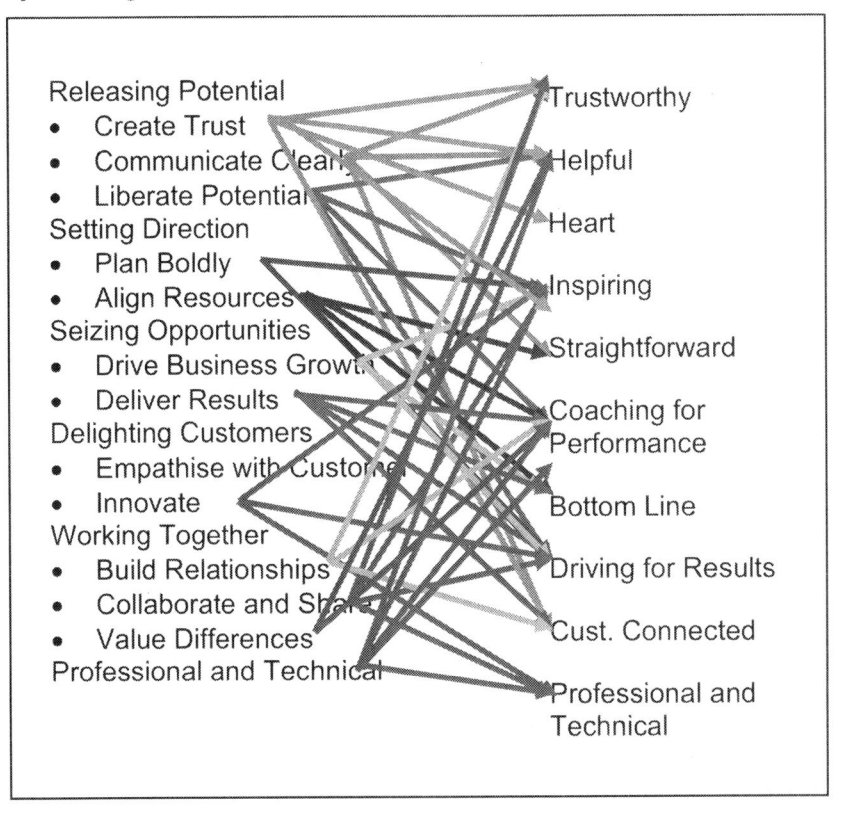

Releasing Potential
- Create Trust
- Communicate Clearly
- Liberate Potential

Setting Direction
- Plan Boldly
- Align Resources

Seizing Opportunities
- Drive Business Growth
- Deliver Results

Delighting Customers
- Empathise with Customers
- Innovate

Working Together
- Build Relationships
- Collaborate and Share
- Value Differences

Professional and Technical

→ Trustworthy
→ Helpful
→ Heart
→ Inspiring
→ Straightforward
→ Coaching for Performance
→ Bottom Line
→ Driving for Results
→ Cust. Connected
→ Professional and Technical

And I thought: what an incomprehensible mess! How can I change my behaviours and map them across. Then I STOPPED! I realised

Success versus Completion – Your Choice

Values

that I have a set of values, these are what are important to me, not the behaviours. These are my Values and they do not change with organisational systems. They are my Paradigm – my pattern, model or perspective.

This made me aware of two things. Firstly, I have a set of values and these do not change whatever the "systems" in use. Secondly, my actions based on my values need little modification to address changes in the assessment systems, processes or techniques used in the organisation where I work.

So, if I am part of some internal Assessment Process and it changes, my values stay the same. My actions are only very slightly modified because they are based primarily on my values and not on the assessment process. So, rather than the Assessment Process driving my Actions (and Values), my Values should drive my Actions - and they both feed into the Assessment Process as follows:

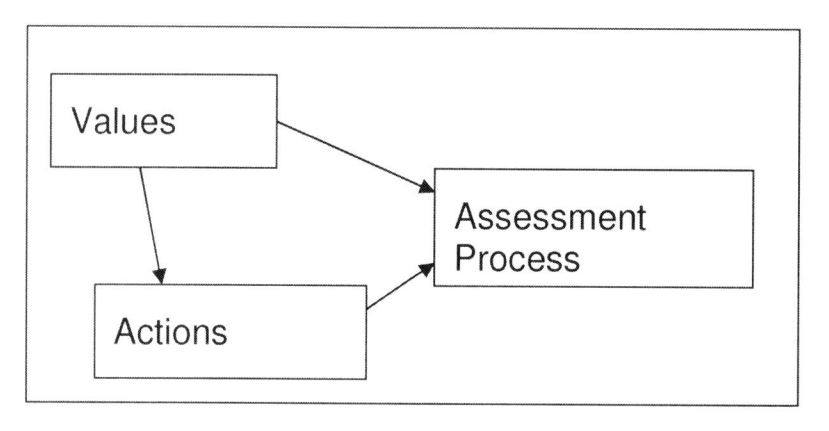

```
┌─────────────────────────────────────────────┐
│   ┌──────────┐                              │
│   │  Values  │──────┐                       │
│   └────┬─────┘      │   ┌──────────────┐   │
│        │            └──▶│  Assessment  │   │
│        ▼                │   Process    │   │
│   ┌──────────┐      ┌──▶└──────────────┘   │
│   │ Actions  │──────┘                       │
│   └──────────┘                              │
└─────────────────────────────────────────────┘
```

This enables me to retain my sanity and remain true to myself.

Your Values may include some of the following and may include many others

- Integrity
- Honesty
- Consistency
- Commitment
- Reliability
- Persistence
- Popularity
- Etc. Etc. Etc.

Success versus Completion – Your Choice

Values are what we strive for, they are ideals or goals for how we live our lives. This does not mean that we always adhere to them, but that we generally strive to achieve them.

So.....

Key Principle

Identify your VALUES

Applying this Key Principle simplifies your life - it gives you an anchor so you are not blown off course by change at work, at home or wherever. As a result, you should be better able to deliver what is expected of you.

Ask yourself the question "What characteristics do I aspire to?"

These are your Values or Ideals - we are (I am) not perfect: we make mistakes, we get it wrong and we hide our mistakes when we should not.

There is an Army Personnel Evaluation Questionnaire which includes the following question:

> What do you do if you hit someone's car when parking at the supermarket?
> A. Pretend it did not happen.
> B. Check if anyone noticed, and, if not, pretend it did not happen.
> C. Leave a note on their windscreen but no contact details.
> D. Leave a note on their windscreen with contact details.

We know what we should do but we do not always do it. However we strive to identify our Values, live up to them and learn from where we fell short so we can do better the next time.

Success versus Completion – Your Choice

EXERCISE - VALUES

There is a section at the end under Personal Focus for you to Identify your Values. Please take some time to review and complete (see Page 104).

Think

THINK about how you approach your work (and life). There is a public service broadcaster in the USA who strives to make the cut and thrust of debate such that you actually have to THINK - not to react to extremism, not to get angry at crassness or stupidity but to THINK.

Φ Part 1 THINK

In a well known children's story, a boy is going to market. On the first day he was sent to buy milk. He bought the milk but then could not bring it home because he had not thought to bring a container, so his mother said he should have brought a bucket. On the second day, he was sent for corn, so he brought a bucket and put the corn in the bucket. But the corn is eaten from the bucket by birds. He is told he should have asked for a paper bag. On the third day, he was sent for butter, but the butter melts through the paper .....

When I was at school my Maths teacher emphasised that we needed to <u>apply the learning and not just follow rules</u>. He said if we go in to an exam and discover there was a question about finding the number of oranges left from a bag of 10 after removing 4, he did not want us saying that we could not do this question because we never did any questions regarding oranges in class, they were always with apples!

Φ Part 2 APPLY the THINKING

Taking what we have learnt, and using it in new situations by applying the lessons (not just following the instructions) is what this book is all about. It is not formulaic learning, like some technical courses offer, but experiential learning. It is this that I call going Outside the Nutshell.

So.....

Key Principle

THINK

Engaging your brain (consciously), learning, growing your capabilities, stepping back and THINKing.

Get a Balance

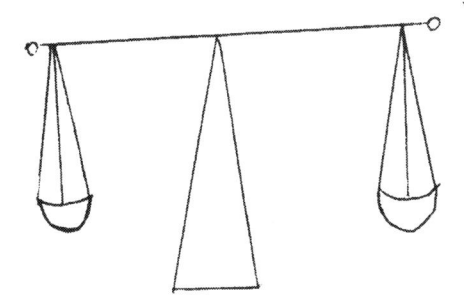

Life and work are not about achieving a single objective at the expense of everything else. Single mindedness can be good but we do not generally abandon everything else for very long and our single mindedness is usually around the fact that other things are taken care of before and after. A woman in labour is single minded but she has (usually!) planned it.

In sport (and war) we are encouraged to be single minded, focus on one objective and pursue it at all costs. There is an army motto that says "If it moves: shoot it; If it is stationary: whitewash it!" Life is not like that (for most of us). Jonathan Edwards (Olympic Triple Jump Champion) said when he retired from athletics that his life will become more complicated. Things are going to pull him in different directions.

Φ Get a BALANCE

This BALANCE has got 2 perspectives. Firstly, it is a balanced approach to tasks. We do not generally achieve anything (let alone everything) in the quickest possible time so plan tasks allowing for contingency and deviations. Secondly, it is a balance across all our tasks. We usually have several or multiple things to do and we have to manage our resources appropriately and change focus as circumstances and results change.

Success versus Completion – Your Choice

Three simple suggestions that I have found helpful in achieving and maintaining this BALANCE are:-

- <u>Seek alternative opinions</u>: Find people whom you trust and respect, that you can be confidential with but do not always see eye to eye with. People who see things differently from you, but also have knowledge in the relevant area. Run your ideas past them. For example if you think you can do a task in 6 months for £100K but you colleague thinks 9 months and £200K and you know you are enthusiastic and optimistic then maybe you should go for £120K and 7 months but if your colleague thinks 4 months and £50K and you know you are cautious and pessimistic then maybe you should go for £80K and 5 months.

- <u>Do not live too near the edge</u>: You will fall over it and there is no room for emergencies or contingency. Your problems become "Self inflicted AND out of your control"!

- <u>Prioritise and act</u>: Do not let things get out of control (this is easier said than done!). When I worked for a software house one of the employees had a sleeping bag in a drawer and another booked flexible holidays. These were always fallen back upon because people knew they were there. This led to the attitude of "I do not have to worry about deadlines because I have a way out". Again your problems become "Self inflicted AND out of your control"!

So…..

Key Principle

Get a BALANCE

Because a slower day is NOT coming, get a BALANCE in your activities and actions **and** across your responsibilities, in both what we do **and** in how we do it.

Success versus Completion – Your Choice

Times and circumstances may dictate changes in priorities and actions but, if we do not exert some control over our own life, we will lose all control and influence and be buffeted about by external demands. So, if you are too busy to do something that you should be doing, or have agreed to do, then you have 3 options:
1. Delegate – action on you
2. Does not need done – action on you to decide this and report (with a reason)
3. Drop something else – action on you to decide and report (with a reason)

You can see that achieving a Balance rests with you! Balance requires people to be flexible and reasonable, not intransigent. We cannot say we have a balanced workload because we spend 10 minutes on every task and we just rotate round the tasks in hand – that is your brain opting out and not THINKing.

Success versus Completion – Your Choice

Know Your Skills

We all have skills, talents and abilities but they are not all the same. Also it is not always what you have but how you respond, not the hand you are dealt but how you play it. In The Lord of the Rings trilogy different people achieved different things, everyone did not achieve the same nor did they have the same capabilities. But you have to know what you have (your hand) to enable you to utilise it to the best benefit and it is not just you but the hand available to you (team, colleagues, equipment, partners, location …….)

Things to ponder (THINK!) in addressing this are what am I good at, what do I like, what is my nature? Do I look for consistency or do I have a desire for change? Am I a Vision and Mission person or a Completeness and Detail person? Do I like to be in control or am I more of a trouble-shooter? Am I a morning person or an afternoon person? Am I socially focused or achievements focused?

Your preferences and your values are also important as well as the life work balance you want to achieve. Remember what you want to do is play to your strengths.

None of the above are good vs bad or better vs best but they are important in finding out your skills and talents.

Success versus Completion – Your Choice

Remember also that competent Project Managers can use most Project Management systems, competent Primary School teachers can adapt to new systems of teaching. Your skills (and those available to you) will transcend most processes (with minor adaptation/modification) – although you may require some extra time to learn and adapt.

But also, avoid navel gazing and "paralysis of self analysis"!

Key Principle

Know your SKILLS

And those not available to you as well!

EXERCISE - SKILLS

There is a section at the end under Personal Focus for you to identify your Skills, Talents and Abilities. Please take some time to review and complete (See Page 106)

Growth

We have the ability to learn. When I was learning to drive a man came out of a shop, crossed the road, got into his car and drove away in the time it took me to get the clutch / accelerator balance – it was demoralising! But that which we persist in doing becomes easier because we grow. I can now drive a car a lot better than I could then.

A colleague once said to me "We do not do schedule plans in this team because we tried it once and it did not work". If we want to grow we have to be prepared to learn, if we want to learn we have to be prepared to not get it right every time, especially the first time.

We should strive to attain our VALUES, and if we do we will attain them more regularly or fall short by less and this will result in GROWTH.

VALUES + Applying the THINKING + BALANCE + SKILLS leads to GROWTH

Look for improvements, look for Growth

Success versus Completion – Your Choice

Key Principle

GROWTH

We can improve.

We will Learn and Grow. Assess what you have done and learn how to do it better next time. This is especially relevant when faced with disappointment and failure. It is important to learn and grow rather than being distressed and shrinking.

Be aware and try to avoid closing the door on aspects, activities or people that have let you down or have caused you distress. Try to assess, learn and be better prepared the next time. The key is to be better prepared not to pretend it never happened.

Remember the
<u>Apply the THINKING Principle</u> – if it did not work the last time and you do the same thing again it probably will not work this time.
<u>Get a BALANCE Principle</u> – you do not have to address every problem every time, sometimes it is better to abandon, work around or leave till later.

Key Principles recap

The Key Principles are

- *1* - Identify your VALUES
- *2* - THINK
- *3* - Get a BALANCE
- *4* – Know Your SKILLS
- *5* – GROW (we can improve)

These are important, we need to remember them and we need to use them. Moving on to HOW! - The Application.

Using what we have learnt – here is how I think we can apply it.

Success versus Completion – Your Choice

Application   Page 33

SECTION 3
APPLICATION

On your marks!   Amber

Success versus Completion – Your Choice

Application

Success versus Completion – Your Choice

Overview

How to survive!!

How to succeed!!

Using the 5 Key Principles and applying to the real world

- Pre-assignment – what to do
- Start up / Initiation / Arrival at a new job, project or assignment
- Initiation to Stability (the first few weeks or months, hopefully!)
- Stability and Building on it
- Finishing, Signing Off and Getting Out
- Success and Failure throughout the cycle

The first three are the most important, if we do not start off right then we are always trying to correct, adjust and re-align because of early mistakes. This is relevant whether you are initiating a new project or joining an existing one, but some of the items will become more relevant or appropriate than others in different circumstances.

A lot of the themes and topics will appear in various sections as they are important in several of the areas but in most cases the application will differ from section to section.

Finally there is a section with Templates and Guides

Application

Success versus Completion — Your Choice

Pre-assignment

Don't go yet!

- *Maryium Nut* – Excellent for preventing heartburn and very healthy.
  Small nut usually overlooked but can be essential in avoiding indigestion later

So what do you need before you start?

- **Objectives**
- **What is Success?**
- **Influence and Concern**
- **Integrity**
- **Learn and Grow**
- **Remain Conscious**

What do you bring to the table/event/project…..?

How should you prepare?

Success versus Completion – Your Choice

Φ Objectives

Find out your Objectives and find out what is expected of you. A delegation list that we will re-visit later may help. Can you answer the following and if not can you find them out?

- *Do you know the results to be achieved?*
  What but not necessarily how
- *Do you have clear guidelines?*
  Including known pit-falls, things that are not allowed and the level of initiative/freedom expected.
- *Do you know what resources are available?*
- *Do you know who you are accountable to?*
  Including when to report progress and what is being used to evaluate progress.
- *Do you know the consequences, both positive and negative?* [1]

If you do not know where you are going then the chances are you will end up somewhere else (or lost!). During the famine in Ireland in the mid-nineteenth century the government, for want of something to do and for lack of any other solution, set men to digging roads with no direction and no purpose. "Building roads that lead to nowhere". Do not make people busy for the sake of it and do not make yourself busy for the sake of it. If you do not know what is expected, then find out.

Φ What is Success?

Be prepared to ask why you are doing what you are doing, do not just ask what to do. Look beyond your objectives. In the Outward Bound example the actual reason for the event is not to do with getting to the destination or enhancing their survival skills. This is exceptional, in nearly all cases the Objectives are core to the

---

[1] Cf **7 Habits of Highly Effective People** by Stephen R. Covey pp 173ff

success but remember that the Objectives are not the only thing that will be used to gauge success.

Ask yourself "Why are these my objectives?" Look for any other items that will affect success. Then you will be better placed to understand what success looks like.

Φ Influence and Concern[2]

Be aware of your influences and concerns

*God Grant Me The Serenity
To Accept The Things I Cannot Change
Courage To Change The Things I Can
And The Wisdom To Know The Difference*

Reinhold Niebuhr 1892 - 1971

Strangely enough the truer we are to this the more our influence grows.

The following model uses 2 circles, the inner one to represent what we have an influence over, and the outer one to represent what we have concern over.

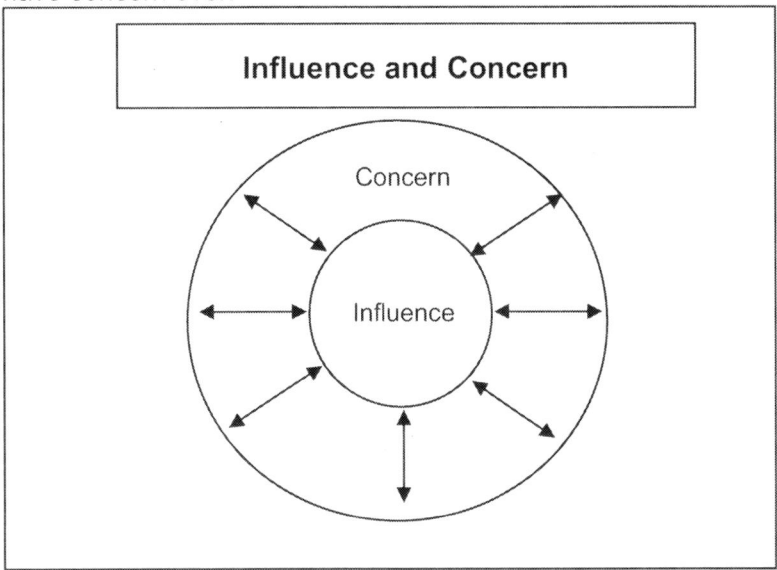

Influence and Concern

(Diagram: outer circle labeled "Concern", inner circle labeled "Influence", with arrows pointing outward from the inner circle)

Our actions can either extend outwards our circle of influence or contract it inwards.

---

[2] Cf **7 Habits of Highly Effective People** by Stephen R. Covey ppP81ff

Success versus Completion – Your Choice

We should strive to achieve a BALANCE. Do not be a door mat and do not be a dictator. If you focus on your Influences and Concerns or if you focus on avoidance of being a door mat or avoidance of being a dictator you will not achieve the best results.

Try to focus on your **VALUES**. Who you are, not who you think others might want you to be! Try to focus on your **SKILLS** and knowing your strengths and weaknesses.

Know what you want to do and find a way that works for you (and the business, and the team,....). Do not find a way that you love if it hinders or undermines the business or people around you!

Be prepared to focus on the whole (not just one aspect of it), addressing all of the following, or as much as possible
- Self
- Team - people working for you
- Project/deliveries/objectives - what you have to do
- Customers and Partners - other companies involved
- Colleagues - people who are not part of your team but who you work with
- The Business or Company you work for

THINK - You will **GROW** (and so will your influence). But also beware of being side-tracked into areas out of your influence or concern and getting caught up in irrelevant work. Focus and re-focus on your aims and objectives so you have the right influence and the right concerns.

Φ Integrity

If only I could fake it…..

Some encouragement towards it!

Firstly: the following actions, which are closely related to VALUES, make a big difference and go a long way to establishing trust and confidence (and consequently integrity).

> *Little things make a big difference, things like courtesy and respect.*

> *Keep your promises (do not break them). Fulfil expectations - irrespective of who they are to.*
>
> *Your honour is greater than your moods. This seems mediaeval but bear it in mind. If you agreed it yesterday but do not feel like doing it today – still do it!*
>
> *Be loyal, especially to those not present*
>
> *Apologise when wrong*

Doing the opposite also goes a very long way to undermine trust and confidence– and undermines integrity and personal reputation.

Secondly: take time to listen and understand.

> "Not hearing the question it was easy for him to give an answer"
>
> Dag Hammarskjold UN Secretary General 1953-1961
>
> If one answers before hearing it is folly and shame
>
> (Pr 18:13)

Thirdly: try to do more than just scratch the surface. Engender trust but do not take everything the way you want to hear it (BALANCE). I was once talking to my son when he was 2 and he was wearing a blue top with orange sleeves. He pointed to one of the sleeves and said "Orange". I thought "Oh my, that is clever, he knows some of his colours". He then pointed to his other sleeve and said "Apple". I then thought "Ah, he has a long way to go". So make sure the answers you get supply you with the information you need.

Fourthly: manage people's expectations. Tell them to let you know if you make a mistake, are about to make a mistake or if they want to alert you to some risk or issue coming up. Otherwise tell them you expect deliveries are going to be on time and as agreed. It avoids the "Why did someone not say earlier" scenario.

Finally: let your "No" mean "No" and your "Yes" mean "Yes". Say it and do it, or do not say it!

Success versus Completion – Your Choice

Φ Learn and GROW

Look at the bigger picture, it helps you to learn and **GROW**, look ahead from time to time, dream. Nobody ever said on their deathbed - "I wish I spent more time at my desk"!

"A man who views the world the same at 50 as he did at 20 has wasted 30 years of his life"

Muhammad Ali

And it is not what you do but how you do it that can make a difference. A survey of nurses giving an injection found the actions of nurses who patients said gave them a positive experience differed very little from those that gave a negative experience, the key difference was that the positive experience came from nurses who sympathised with the patients pain and discomfort and the negative experience came with those nurses that did not - both groups of nurses were quick, efficient and applied the injection successfully.[3]

So dream (from time to time!) – be prepared to step "Outside the Nutshell". Ask yourself what you want the future to look like – engage people in it and why you are doing it and get their input.

---

[3] Cf **Break all the Rules** by Buckingham and Coffman, published by Simon and Schuster (pp 93-94)

Φ Remain Conscious

Use your common sense and your experience, do not switch off and follow processes blindly. If you press the buttons on a calculator and get the answer 45.237 for the Square Root of 14 you know it is wrong.

If it is in an exam where calculators are not necessary then you investigate why you had to find the square root of 14 in the first place! We need to apply the same reasoning in our day-to-day jobs. Do not let circumstances alone dictate priorities - ask why? Ask what should I be doing?

If something overruns, make a conscious decision about your response

If you have 3 simultaneous events in your diary it is not good, although a lot of people might think it is! Make a decision, delegate and apologise. If you have 3 simultaneous events regularly, then things are out of control. Take action to rectify. Prioritise (part of **BALANCE**).

THINK - things overrun, they always do. Do not expect to live on the edge, it is not Hollywood and no-one is going to make an action/thriller/blockbuster about your life - so do not worry about keeping your audience on tenterhooks. Try to get off the treadmill and manage a way out.

EXERCISE - OBJECTIVES

Success versus Completion — Your Choice

Pre-assignment   Page 44

There is a section at the end under Personal Focus for you to identify your Objectives. Please take some time to review and complete (See Page 110)

Φ **Recap**: Things to look at and THINK about before you start on an assignment

- Objectives
- What is Success?
- Influence and Concern
- Integrity
- Learn and Grow
- Remain Conscious

This has been preparatory, looking at what you should be thinking about before you engage.

Where are we going and what is our mission?

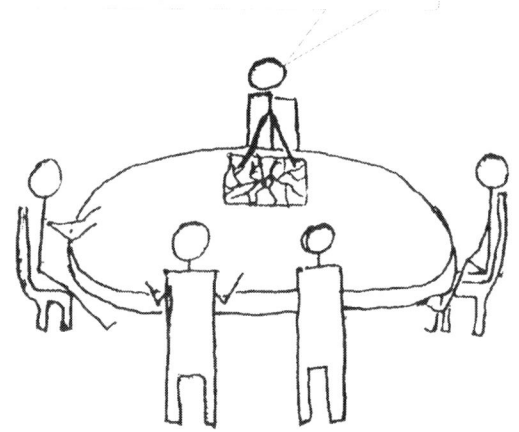

Success versus Completion – Your Choice

Start-Up

> *Kevinut – Sweet and tasty. Usually rushed when it should be eaten slowly and properly*

Your project is starting or you are arriving at a new project. What is important? Building on the Pre-assignment preparation we will be looking at

- **Project Management**
- **Project Activities**
- **Making Progress**
- **Resources**
- **Delegation and Reporting**
- **Team Management**

You should have some clarity of what you are trying to achieve and what the overall objectives are as you go through the Start Up.

Success versus Completion – Your Choice

Φ Project Management

Plan, plan and plan - and plan for deviations to the plan. If it is a complex piece of work ensure you have a robust, tried and tested project management system in place.

Integrity is key to project success. A survey of project managers that had successfully delivered 3 consecutive major projects found that the common factor was ***integrity.*** They were either very good or very lucky - either case I want them to manage my projects!

So do not just chase the next big win, the next big issue or the next big revenue at the expense of other things (or everything). Plan ahead, identify your end goal, ask what are the consequences? Do not accept "let's get the major issue out of the way and then look at the consequences." The consequences will never be looked at as another major issue will appear (and another and another…).

Identify the key players - this is not just the high profile ones like the Finance Director and the Account Manager but also the people that make the business tick. Find out what people's roles and responsibilities are, step back and think and support and engage them.

Having an agreed level of service is good – but it is not worth doing if you cannot report on it and prove compliance or otherwise. This is the case for both your work and for those whom you rely upon.

The web is a great facility for sharing data but if you are using it make sure you maintain it and keep it up to date.

But, but, but, but….Processes are not enough, a formulaic approach where you do not know why you are doing something will put you in trouble.

> *A Project I was on had a Risks and Issues call every Monday afternoon because that was in the manual, but it was just a talking shop, no-one was called to task and nothing ever got closed. After 3 months there were over 100 open Risks and Issues, the call was lasting over 3 hours and at the Project Board that became the biggest project Risk!!!*

Success versus Completion – Your Choice

Start-Up   Page 47

We need to know why we are doing things and what the objectives are, remember the train story at the start.

Seat 12A wants a Laphroaig Whisky - So I am going to get one

Take time out and make yourself available, listen to peoples' issues. Always visit the coal face - find out what it is like (if at all possible). Make contact face to face and follow up, do not overly rely on processes especially if they are only word of mouth and not visible. Visit your team (they appreciate it), visit the customer (they love it), visit the end user, they do not expect it but it gives them a forum for issues, gets buy in and commitment and gives you the opportunity to address their requirements even if they are not directly tasked or funded.

Do not just manage by exception, make sure you are also keeping to plan. Walk in another man's shoes, THINK and ask questions because there is nothing like experience and nothing like experiencing another perspective. There was an HMI school inspection that recommended 95% of pupils go on work experience but the school only had an 80% attendance record! This undermined the whole schools confidence in the inspectors because they failed to grasp the school's circumstances.

Success versus Completion – Your Choice

Try to be generous. Sacrifice can bring progress. An unselfish act directed at others without expectation of return can transform people and situations. So use the carrot and the stick – the stick on its own does not work even if you have been given all the authority you need!

"Service to others is the rent you pay for your room here on earth"
Muhammad Ali

Keep things simple. Life, work and circumstances are complicated enough and throw up enough obstacles, do not accept, plan in or adopt extra complications, solutions that are not essential or technology that is not proven or does not deliver a benefit. When I worked for the Ambulance Service I had the following conversation when implementing an IT system:

> Control Room Operator: "What do we do when the patient is not at the pick up point?"
>
> Me: Immediately thinking of an IT / system solution, extra requirements, extra work, delays etc. etc. replied with the inspired question "What do you normally do"
>
> Operator: "Radio the Ambulance and tell them"
>
> Me: "Just keep doing that when the new system comes in"

Also find out the other persons thoughts, perspectives, concerns and scratch below the surface. There was a minister who could not work out why a member of the congregation who attended every week never came forward for communion. The problem was causing the minister sleepless nights between a belief the parishioner was avoiding him and a growing concern that there was some very serious problem and his imagination was beginning to run riot as to what it could be. Eventually courage and opportunity coincided and he asked what the problem was, the parishioner sheepishly replied that he had holes in the soles of his shoes and was too embarrassed to kneel at the altar and let all the other parishioners see he could not afford new shoes.

So do not jump to conclusions.

Success versus Completion – Your Choice

If you manage to address the above at the start up then you will be on your way to establishing a good project environment but do not forget to follow them and to continue to follow them throughout the project.

Φ Project Activities

This is not so much project management but project related activities that help support the project.

Take initiative, be pro-active and support other people's actions. Your objective should not be to delegate all actions but to do for others as you would like others to do for you **(BALANCE)**.

At meetings and discussions keep a note of your actions and those of others that are relevant and follow up on your own actions. Do not wait for minutes, do not wait for the next meeting and say "I do not remember this can someone explain", instead be responsible and accountable, lead from the front - it prompts others to follow your example.

Don't go down blind alleys that have already been investigated and failed. Find out what went before. When I worked with a supplier every new assignee stated that they did not know what had gone before and could I bring them up to date, but this implies their company does not care and has made no effort at a handover.

Use Contractors and Professionals as they can be an excellent investment but you need to review, assess and interview or they will take advantage, just keep seats warm for no value and bring in their second division.

Be aware of your audience, whether it is managers, contractors, colleagues, team, sales force, technical people, support people, your mother-in-law.....**DO NOT** tell a salesman your budget **OR** tell a consultancy firm your problems unless you are willing for them to present a costed proposal to fix them to your line manager (or project sponsor!) within 24 hours!

If you can't do something - do something about it, do not leave it alone.

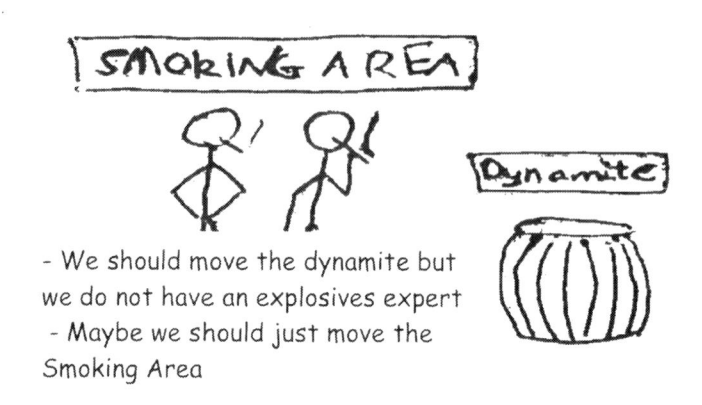

SMOKING AREA

- We should move the dynamite but we do not have an explosives expert
- Maybe we should just move the Smoking Area

I believe that it was Pope John Paul II who said "Peace is not just the absence of war but the fruit of justice". We should bear this in mind - success is the fruit of addressing our issues, concerns and problems not the fact that we do not have any. We should identify potential problems and have a plan of action to address them. We should have a contingency in place (time, budget and resource) to address unidentified problems. We should be reasonable (BALANCED) in how we plan and respond. We should **not** quote timescales and budget based on optimistic, problem and issue free estimates but we also should **not** quote timescales and budget based current problems and issues. We **should** quote timescales and budget based on experience and that new problems and issues will probably surface to add to the current ones.

Φ Making Progress

Agreeing objectives is easier than creating them.

It is easier to progress a proposal than to create one from scratch. Although you get more criticism as the author than you do as the mediator you also get quicker progress than if you get everyone round the table with a blank canvas!

Φ Resources

Recognise differences between people and build on them because the team needs all types of SKILLS. So try to use your resources wisely by knowing your strengths and weaknesses and managing them, utilise your skill base and play to your strengths not your weaknesses. Remember people do not change that much so try to draw out what is left in, do not try to add what was left out but be **very** careful, do **not** assume people are incapable of learning or growing.

Try answering the following two questions.

Question 1 - Prioritise the following attending at the scene of an accident

- First rate paramedic with second rate Ambulance
- First rate paramedic with first rate Ambulance
- Second rate paramedic with second rate Ambulance
- Second rate paramedic with first rate Ambulance

Question 2
   a) On an outward bound trip which would you choose?
   - First rate equipment
   - Second rate equipment
   b) On an outward bound trip which would you choose?
   - First rate equipment with vague objectives
   - Second rate equipment with clear objectives

Generally people are our assets, not systems or equipment and clear objectives are better than equipment.

But remember to scratch below the surface. Do not be like the Andre Previn sketch on The Morcambe and Wise show and realise too late when Eric Morecame says "I **am** playing all the right notes...but not necessarily in the right order". Or like the company I worked for where the person who was backing up the companies data every night thought the message that said "tape finished" meant the backup was complete, whereas what it meant was there is no space for data on the tape – this went on undetected for 6 months!!

Start-Up   Page 52

[Cartoon: Two stick figures outside a "JOB ASSIGNMENT" office. One says "I got sent to Lapland, you?" The other replies "Australia!"]

So use your resources wisely and manage them.

Φ Delegation[4] and Reporting

Delegation saves time in the long term and empowers others. It should be based on a clear understanding and a mutual commitment to succeed, try to address:

- Results to be achieved - what but not how
- Guidelines are set clearly, known pit-falls, "no-no's" and levels of initiative and freedom
- Resources that are available
- Accountability, when to report progress and the standards for evaluating results
- Consequences both positive and negative

When reporting and asking for progress reports the following outlines levels of freedom or initiative:

---

[4] Cf **7 Habits of Highly Effective People** by Stephen R. Covey pp 173ff

Success versus Completion – Your Choice

- Wait till told - No initiative, for raw recruits
- Ask - At least has the initiative to ask
- Recommend - Coming up with suggestions
- Act and Report immediately - Ensure actions were right immediately
- Act and Report routinely - e.g. weekly meetings

Φ Team Management

When leading or managing a team protect them, listen to them and ask advice of them. Make sure they know what they are doing, their roles and responsibilities and their objectives. Also give people a role/job and responsibilities not just actions and tasks. Do not have a "solve the next problem" attitude, as people will lose heart if all you do is hand out tasks to get over the next hurdle. There is no knowledge build up or responsibility and it leads to discouragement and disinterest.

Also remember high expectation and encouragement help people believe in themselves. Your team also appreciates it when you do things early and not always last minute, when you engage them regularly and when you manage the job and the responsibilities and not just the issues. It is also important to take time out and sharpen the saw so that you and your team can cut down more trees in less time than the guy who does not take a break.

Appreciate that when on a new assignment it takes longer to get up to speed so start with high commitment and then level out, do not start part time, and it is OK to have lower expectations at the start. When I was helping my sister learn to drive I realised that much as everyone expected her to talk to the passengers and drive she was not yet in the position to do that but it would come eventually.

But much as the above are important remember that you will primarily be measured on delivery, so deliver, deliver and deliver and then prove it and articulate it.

Success versus Completion – Your Choice

Start-Up   Page 54

Exercise – Start-Up

There is a section at the end under Personal Focus for you to review Start Up. Please take some time to review and complete (see Page 114)

Φ **Recap:** Things to look at and THINK about during assignment start up:

- Project Management
- Project Activities
- Making Progress
- Resources
- Delegation and Reporting
- Team Management

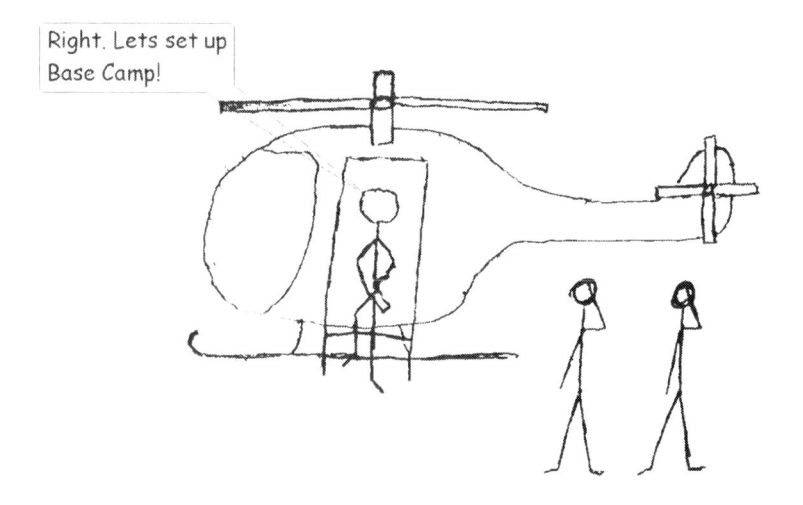

Right. Lets set up Base Camp!

Success versus Completion – Your Choice

Initiation to Stability

- *Peternut* – Very soft shell, easy to open but also very easy to damage the nut inside in the process.

You have started up, you think you know what you want to do…So what are the keys to reaching stability?

- ***Teamwork***
- ***Detours***
- ***Partners***

Φ Teamwork

As mentioned earlier Teamwork is very, very important, do not underestimate it, either the potential of having it or the consequences of not having it.

"Remember" Pull not Push

Vince Lombardi once said "People who work together will win whether it is against complex football defences or problems of modern society" ...or projects deliverables!!!

Teamwork involves everyone, not just your immediate team.

Also remember that today's adversary may well be tomorrow's ally **(BALANCE)**. So do not alienate people when you have issues but try to accommodate and compromise because the same people may want to support you in tomorrow's issues. Do not try to be like radio phone ins which try to polarise and highlight extremes. They do not help to reach satisfactory conclusions. We live in an interdependent society, so seeking alternative opinions is good. It is good to discuss with both your opponent and your ally as it helps to reach a solution suitable for everybody but remember this does not mean you always have to compromise.

We are subjective, recognise it and undertake to address it, but it cannot be self-corrected, we need others to assist us. This is where convincing other people helps us to iron out our glitches and mistakes.

Also in working with other people bear in mind that if you do something once you will be expected to do it again, the following may help emphasise the point.

Previous experiences or results dictate current expectations, for example...

- *An Industrial Tribunal found in favour of a man appealing against a sacking after his fourth final written warning because the actions of the previous three had implied the same actions for the fourth i.e. no sacking!*

Success versus Completion – Your Choice

- *There was a training course where the equipment did not work the previous time and the trainers were surprised it did not work again – you should expect it not to work and take corrective action in advance.*

Along the same theme it is also important to remember you cannot talk yourself out of a situation you have acted yourself into. If someone promises something 3 times and does not deliver each time (e.g. being on time or completing an action) and promises it a fourth time – be prepared for them not to do it irrespective of how much they try to convince you they will do it. If we do things regularly others will expect us to continue and if others do things regularly expect them to continue and let them know it!

Teamwork involves discussing what to expect, agreeing to it, doing it and discussing the outcome afterwards.

Work together so as be a team player outside your company as well as within it. Seek a win-win result, but bear in mind it is not always achievable and it is not always available. To help to do this try to understand the consequences of your actions and encourage others to do likewise. It is not thinking outside of the box but getting out of your box by putting your head above the parapet and see what is going on. Try to see the consequences for those working with you, for those working for you and those working around you by stepping "Outside the Nutshell".

Some good examples of this are

- *An Obstetrician who was delivering quadruplets said he had a difficult decision because one of them was not progressing well and he had to decide when to deliver via caesarean section. He pointed out that if one of the babies died in the womb it would be his fault but if the babies died after delivery it would be the paediatrician's fault. He said it was difficult to stand back and make the decision based on the best for the babies (and mother) rather than make the decision based on what would be the least likely for blame to come back to him.*
- *Ceasefires in areas of conflict increases the intensity of the warfare up until the ceasefire comes into operation because the agreed ceasefire date and time is generally used to*

define the boundaries going forward for the factions involved. Much as this may not be relevant in business it does have a business equivalent..

- *If you withdraw a product temporarily because prices are too low and you inform your sales force in advance then you create a short term market frenzy as the sales team use it to boost their sales by telling the customer the prices are increasing.*

So get out of your box and understand the consequences of your actions, be responsible and encourage others to do likewise. Be visible and available, do not hide behind emails, messages and memos.

Do not give knee jerk reactions especially when something has aggravated you. It can be helpful to compose a response but not to send it immediately, come back to it later and re-read it before sending or calling because the chances are either the situation gets resolved or an hours delay enables you to be much more constructive.

Φ Detours

They will happen and they will be when you least expect. But you should have planned for deviations to the plan and for changes in requirements and objectives (see Page 50).

Deviations can also be instigated by people issues and events that take you or your resources away (e.g. an Outward bound team building event at short notice!).

But remember the law of diminishing returns, there will always be exceptions, contradictions and difficulties. When I worked for the Scottish Ambulance Service whenever someone came up with a new process, guidelines or management statistic to be gathered the Senior Officer in charge of the North of Scotland would nearly always say "It will never work in Bettyhill". This was a remote (north west corner) ambulance station that was a law unto itself. At the end of the day most decisions were made without implementation at Bettyhill, its size, location and use meant it did not affect performance statistics anyway, the local community were more than satisfied with the service they were getting and it was only really worth making an issue for legal, operational or health and safety issues.

So do not spend your time trying to address peripheral problems that do not seriously affect the overall success of the engagement. Remember the law of diminishing returns.

Also when detours present themselves seek advice, it is out there. You do not need all the answers, you only need to know how to find the answers.

And remember when things change and this requires extra effort then this has consequences, so, if you can, publish the consequences up front because if you do something once you will be expected to do it again (and again and again).

Φ Partners

Working with partners, people from another company or another department, can be very contentious especially if you are not used to it. Something that really helps is to identify their objectives, ask yourself what you would do in their position (**THINK**). They want to generate revenue for their company or success for their department and this is OK but do not forget it, good partners want to generate revenue and success for you as well. You should also ask what do the partners bring to the table? Think about it and try to be objective.

The following is taken from my experience of bringing a consultancy firm into a large corporation.

- *The things we discovered they were good at were managing the customer, commercial awareness, rapid resource response, financial reporting and securing funds. They showed a great confidence at Initiation and had a "Can do, will do" attitude. They focused on deliveries and made them happen, they drove the project forward and showed great confidence to achieve. They were also not bogged down by internal issues and politics.*

- *The things they were not so good at were they had an **in**ability to understand our company's way of working, they were dictatorial and expected to be in charge, these two issues resulted in them paying scant regard to our company's regulations let alone guidance, best practice or quality and getting them to adhere to our Quality Gates was a joke.*

- *Our conclusion was that when dealing with partners remember they can have two faces one for customer and one for supplier, they spend full time and more on customer management but they should not be on a pedestal - they are real people.*

The above is only an example, I am trying to emphasise that there are pros and cons. Partners can be very helpful and very supportive if managed right and with the right buy in from senior management. It is especially important to assess why they are being brought in, what they bring to the table both positive and negative, what objectives they are set and what objectives they will have set themselves.

EXERCISE – INITIATION TO STABILITY

There is a section at the end under Personal Focus for you to review Initiation to Stability. Please take some time to review and complete (see Page 118)

Initiation to Stability

Φ **Recap:** Considerations as you move towards stability
- Teamwork
- Detours
- Partners

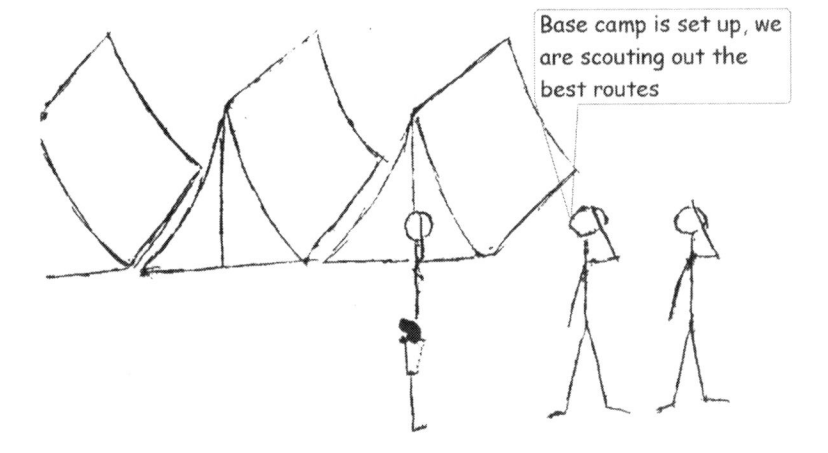

> Base camp is set up, we are scouting out the best routes

Success versus Completion – Your Choice

Stability and Building on it

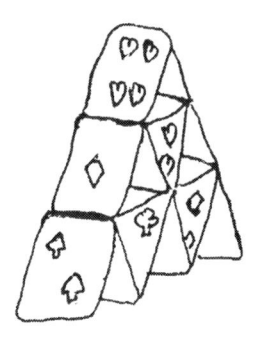

- *Plainus nut – Easy to open but very plain tasting on its own.*
- *Jay Jay nut – Needs time and effort to open but taken in small quantities with the Plainus nut gives a very satisfying taste.*

You have started up, hit all the initial problems and issues and have now settled into business as usual. How do you maintain stability and how do you build on it?

- **Team Building**
- **Team Player**
- **Correcting Mistakes**
- **Celebrate Success and Achievements**
- **Skills**
- **Leadership**

Success versus Completion – Your Choice

Φ Team Building

Again do not underestimate teamwork but Stability brings a slightly different focus. "Give a man a fish and he eats for a day, teach a man to fish and he eats for a lifetime". We have to let people **GROW**

Great managers are not looking for people that are easy to manage, this should not be on their agenda, they should be looking for the people who have the talent to stand out, especially once they have passed the project initiation stage.

We need to let people learn and achieve. In Charles Dickens' Bleak House[5] he tells of Mrs Bagnet's birthday meal. He describes how a Mr Bagnet always makes the dinner on the occasion of his wife's birthday, a tradition for over 15 years. Much as it is a treat for the wife there are drawbacks…

"As he is not illustrious for his cookery, this may be a matter of state rather than enjoyment on the old girl's part; but she keeps her state with all imaginable cheerfulness"

She is also very aware of the offence she would cause by interfering on what he sees as his special treat for her. So …

"… itching to prevent what she sees going wrong….(To her children) Mrs Bagnet occasionally imparts a wink, or a shake of the head, or a crooked face, as they make mistakes"

"It is well for the old girl that she has but one birthday in a year…"

And on clearing up after the meal

"The great delight and energy with which the two young ladies (her daughters) apply themselves to these duties … inspires the highest hopes for the future, but some anxiety for the present"

---

[5] Bleak House by Charles Dickens Penguin Classics pp722-723

My father told a story about when he was a boy, one of the women in the village died. She had the reputation as a good and efficient housewife and she would be missed in the community. The day after her death my father saw her son (in his mid twenties) walking towards him along the street. As he approached my father thought he was looking strange, when he got within 50 yards it looked as if he had received a terrible beating as his face was covered in blood but he did not look in any pain or discomfort. On closer inspection it turned out that the blood was all superficial and had been caused by a first attempt to shave (with an open razor!). The problem was that the mother never had the patience or time to let her son learn to shave as she could not bear to watch him take ten minutes when she could do it in five. So she had shaved him every day of his adult life!

We have to let people learn, we have to take the angst of Mrs Bagnet and overcome the impatience and poor quality (and rework) that it presents us with in the short term so that the long term benefits are realised.

Φ Team Player

As well as team building remember to be a team player. Sometimes it means - expect the best and plan for the worst. Be positive - it extends your circle of influence into the circle of concern but beware of dictating.

You can only take being helpful so far and then you have to back off or you become interfering and even if you were right people will not appreciate it.

I was once trying to encourage a colleague into resolving a problem. They did not take my advice but afterwards said "I will not ignore your advice again" and said it publicly!

Success versus Completion – Your Choice

Being a Team Player also requires us to probe and question. Invest time in keeping track of other's deliverables where relevant or appropriate. Scratch below the surface and try to understand what other people are doing, committing to and trying to achieve.

Φ Correcting Mistakes

Mistakes should generally be corrected, if we ignore them not only will they not go away but they will be repeated. But correction should always be in private unless the action undermines the team or project. Only then should it be in public. An example would be when the operations team decided to cancel a deployment without reference to the project manager yet publicised this to everyone. I insisted that they withdraw their announcement and acknowledge that it is the project manager who makes the decision so that nobody else thought that it was all right to take a similar action, but I first contacted the person responsible in private, discussed it with them and told them what I was going to do and what I expected them to do.

Always err on correction in private if you are unsure.

Φ Celebrate Success and Achievements

Look for opportunities to celebrate success and do not be frozen by fear of missing someone out.

Learn from your mistakes rather than never doing and never learning, like the example of the young man shaving earlier it will never turn out right or perfect first time but it will improve and it will get easier.

Φ Skills

Use the skills that are available, acknowledge diversity as it enhances productivity. The more exclusive you are the more you limit potential and consequently limit the productivity.

The more you go for an easy life the more work you have to do, the more angst you experience and the less you achieve. So work to encourage and enhance the skills of those around you. But remember competence requires 3 things, it requires ability, instruction and desire. Different tasks and different people will need different amounts but all 3 are necessary. So if a person does not have all three then don't keep letting them fail and don't be like in George Orwell's 1984 and find peoples' biggest nightmare and then identify it as an area of growth - that is actually worse than the rats in 1984!

But also encourage people in the areas they seem to have the ability and the desire in and commit to giving them or getting them the instruction. Too often people are restricted because we are unwilling to invest time in them.

Φ Leadership

A bad leader the people despise
A good leader the people love
A great leader the people say **"We did it ourselves"**
Lao Tzo 600 B.C.

If you are in leadership remember the buck stops with you, even if you have "sub-contracted" or it is out of your control. Remember also that processes do not always assist and resource management does not always help. So know where you are going because people will want to know and if you do not know where you are going then the chances are you will end up lost.

If you are leading then ensure you have a channel to address issues but use it wisely, do not have someone saying your problems are self inflicted. I was in a situation where people did not like the current project set up and complained of everything and took issue with every problem - the result was that the management said **they** were the problem because they were complaining about so many trivial items. Complaints should really only be in humour. If you have a problem with something then note the problem and suggest ideas and solutions, be pro-active and support a change rather than demand an improvement from someone else that cannot be quantified.

Whether or not you are in a position of leadership the following will help

- Choose your battleground. Apologise when wrong, it works better for everyone. Take issue with real issues and not with

Success versus Completion – Your Choice

petty ones and remember winning an argument is not a good enough reason for starting it.

- Err on "Under promise and over achieve". Don't "Over promise and under achieve", the best is "Promise and achieve" *(BALANCE)*
- Unfortunately being right is not good enough and neither is being good. You have to report it, track it, prove it and build on it.

EXERCISE – STABILITY AND BUILDING ON IT

There is a section at the end under Personal Focus for you to review Stability and Building on it. Please take some time to review and complete (see Page 122)

Φ **Recap:** Stability and Building on it

- Team Building
- Team Player
- Correcting Mistakes
- Celebrate Success and Achievements
- Skills
- Leadership

We know the best route like the back of our hands and we know the alternatives if we have any problems

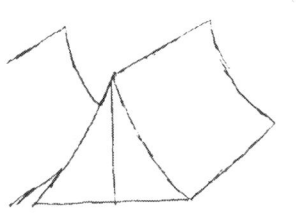

Success versus Completion – Your Choice

Finishing

> *Fergnut – Bittersweet nut also usually overlooked, has an initial bitter taste but leaves a very pleasant after taste.*

How do you finish?

This is a short section but very, very important!

- **Plan the Conclusion**
- **Implement the Plan**
- **Sign off!**
- **De-Brief**

Success versus Completion – Your Choice

Φ Plan the Conclusion

If there is no plan to finish or handover then it will not happen, this is the same as in any phase of an engagement. So THINK:-

- What do you need to do?
- What are the handover criteria?
- Can you have an overlapping assignment where you can support the handover but let someone else do most of the work?
- Do you need to phase people and resources in and do you need to phase other people and resources out?
- What is the cut off date you are aiming for and is it reasonable for everyone involved?
- Is the plan achievable?

Φ Implement the Plan

Once you have planned the conclusion you still need to deliver, deliver, deliver. So follow through and make sure loose ends are sorted.

Remember that you will not be there to pick them up and you do not want to be called back in. Much as your ego likes the initial request to come back the medium and long term consequences are very painful and inhibiting.

I worked for a software house where the newest people were put onto the latest technology and the longest serving and most experienced people were left to maintain the oldest systems because they had never handed them over.

This also results in the triple headache of new people, new project and new technology which is a recipe for problems.

So avoid being forced into it by not being free or by not being able to free up your best or most experienced people

Φ Sign Off

Have a definite finish even if you need some flexibility. Preferably have another activity to move to even if it is training or catching up on background activities.

Close off loose ends.

Celebrate and thank everyone involved.

Φ De-brief

What do you do when it is over? Stop and **THINK**, take some time out. Ask yourself what have you learnt?

Re-read this book and re-do the Exercises!

If you were there again what would you do? Laugh at the mistakes that you made or try to help people to avoid them? Or would you say "Never Again"?

Again remember to identify successes and failures, whether as a team or as an individual and think about how you can avoid the failures and build on the successes.

EXERCISE – FINISHING

There is a section at the end under Personal Focus for you to review Finishing. Please take some time to review and complete (see Page 126)

Success versus Completion – Your Choice

Finishing   Page 72

Φ Recap: How do you finish

- Plan the Conclusion
- Implement the Plan
- Sign off!
- De-Brief

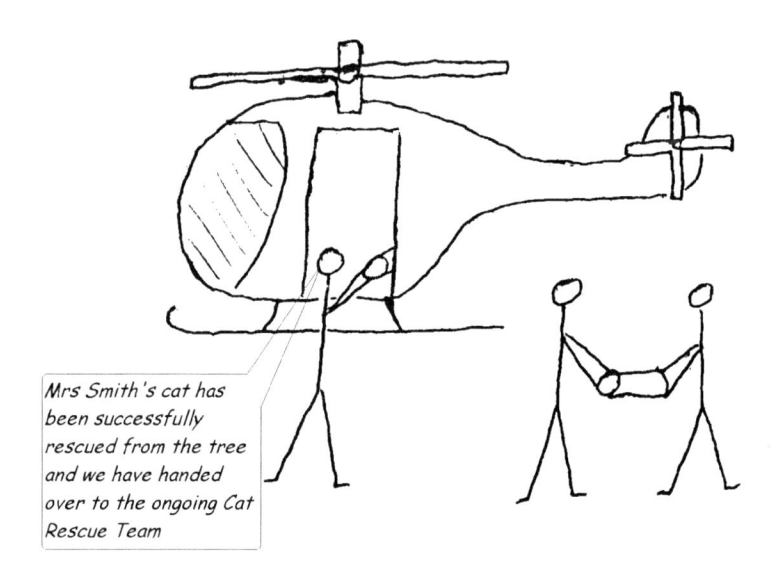

Mrs Smith's cat has been successfully rescued from the tree and we have handed over to the ongoing Cat Rescue Team

Success versus Completion – Your Choice

Success and Failure

The cat is rescued but... Is it alive? Is the tree damaged? Is Mrs Smith happy? Did anyone get hurt? Did the neighbours complain?

- *Brendannut – Has a rock hard shell that is very hard to crack open but is very tasty, usually left alone resulting in numerous unfinished bags of mixed nuts.*

As we move towards a conclusion let us look at some items around success and failure and good and bad practices. These do not fit into a particular phase as they apply across it. We are going to look at:

- **Success and Failure**
- **Process Monkey!**
- **Statistics**
- **Building Relationships**

Success versus Completion – Your Choice

Φ Success and Failure

Mistakes help us to re-align our actions and sometimes our values but if every mistake makes us change our values then we are in trouble. Success can also go to our heads and cause problems and subsequently result in failure!

Bear in mind that overnight success takes a lot of time and effort! If you do not appreciate this then failure may well be more likely. I once heard Frank Dick the ex head of UK Athletics talk about motivation. He used an example from Formula One motor racing and he showed an excerpt from a race. You see a car coming in for a pit stop, it stops, the mechanics start changing the wheel and refuelling. All of a sudden there is a massive fireball and everyone jumps backs, except the marshals who jump forward and extinguish the blaze very quickly and nobody is seriously hurt.

It is very impressive but Frank Dick then said he wanted to play it again and he wanted us to listen very carefully to the commentary. So we do and we hear Murray Walker saying "Oh No! There's a massive fireball, this has never happened before." His point was that although the marshals had never had to deal with this before, and there must be scores of marshals at each race, and there are 20 races a season, they had trained and prepared and knew exactly who should react and what to do because they were responsible for safety in whatever way that it presented itself on the day. The overnight success of those marshals was based on a lot of hard work and dedication and all the marshals at all the races could take pride in them.

So if you want success you have to be prepared to work for it…

> "Dictionary is the only place where success comes before work".
>
> Vince Lombardi

> "Fight is won in the gym and on the road far away from the lights and the ring"
>
> Muhammad Ali

Success versus Completion – Your Choice

Another key aspect of success is not to compare like for like but to compare benefit for benefit AND drawback with drawback. Let me use the following examples.

Do not say the current system, equipment, people have the following drawbacks, if we change to another process, product or team these will be addressed. They will be addressed, if you are right, but what does that bring with it.

If I say my current car (a mini) is cramped, uncomfortable, not the most reliable and if it is in an accident likely to come off worst and I want a replacement - I will end up with a Rolls Royce that is spacious, luxurious, reliable and very, very safe in an accident. But I will have lost my benefits of being cheap, economical and good around town. I will not be able to afford to run it, service it, pay for it or insure it.

We would not dream of doing this with our car but sometimes we do this in our projects and work. We latch on to the complaints and issues and do not look at the current benefits, advantages and usages. There are also a lot of projects that address the problems identified during initiation at the expense of the reason for starting them in the first place and there are a lot of projects that should have been canned at initiation but carry on to completion that are destined to be failures because of the above circumstances.

Φ Process Monkey!

Have you ever been here or have you only experienced this from the outside or from someone else? One of the symptoms is having a "Tick in the Box" mentality. This is all process and no skill or confidence.

- Write your request and we will reply in 24 hours
- But I want the next train to Cardiff!

It sacrifices tomorrow for today and can sometimes seem like having your head in sand and hoping it all goes away. One example that I have come across is having deliveries based on a schedule plan and nothing else, there are no other definitions or more details. I regularly had discussions around "This was not what I had expected" because a schedule plan does not give enough details of what is being delivered or expected and what was delivered did not match expectations.

Another example is what I call dissolving issues, trying to deflect problems or issues, hoping they go away and stalling at every opportunity. I was working on a project and it took me 4 weeks to get someone to admit they were not delivering certain items. The first week I was told that I had the wrong version of the schedule plan and the latest version would be sent to me. The second week I was told that the version I was sent was still the wrong version and the latest version would again be sent to me. The third week I was told that actually the version you had last week was right and the most recent one that was sent is wrong. On the fourth week I finally got them to admit there were quite a few deliveries that were not being made!

We can find ourselves in a "get the job done today and don't address the future" attitude. I have seen people continually request renewals of evaluation licenses when there should have been an order for a bona fide license. I have regularly seen an over promise and fail to achieve, trying to tell people what they want to hear and hope that the problems will go away before you are exposed.

Some things I find helpful in addressing this are to tackle the deployment and implementation issues up front, ensure processes are defined **and** adhered to (e.g. Quality Gates), have a clear focus for any meetings and do not let them become a talking shop.

I also find if I can avoid doing certain things it really helps as well. The things to avoid include regularly failing to attend meetings or calling off at the last minute, having an attitude of "it was not my fault or responsibility so I did not do anything about it" and saying "let's get the contract signed and worry about whether it will work later".

Also - **THINK** what does it look like to other people, especially customers. Get out of your box and think about other people's perspectives. A great antidote is **DON'T DO IT YOURSELF** and a very helpful way of avoiding the process monkey and enhancing the

chances of success are to identify why things are being done and the "spirit" of it, to maintain a vision of the big picture and explain it before explaining the rules and processes. An example is when the Senior Management banned smoking at the Ambulance Service they sent out an article explaining all the rules and with one line at the end explaining why, whereas they should have tried to win people over with the reason before explaining the details.
Remember - without vision the people perish.

Try to make tactical decisions for the benefit of the overall strategy, not the other way round. Water takes the path of least resistance, do we? Or do we take the path of biggest benefit? Sometimes it is uphill and against the flow.

Do not live too near the edge (remember to remain conscious, see Page 43) and remember to sharpen the saw and take time out. Know what is expected and keep a track of deliverables affecting you.

Φ Statistics

"There are lies, damned lies and ....Statistics"
                    Mark Twain

Statistics can be helpful but beware of relying on them because we live in an ever increasing impersonal society where we are obsessed with measuring what is good and what is bad.

ACME INC.

Performance Report

On time   100%

Not on time   0%

Projects surveyed 1

Projects not surveyed 499
(because they did not finish)

Recall the train story at the start. Try to imagine the regional manager of a train company who wants to improve performance and customer satisfaction. They call a meeting of all the station managers. It is much easier for them to take a short amount of time and demand and encourage all station managers to meet the target of 95% of trains leaving on time and motivate them by saying their bonus will be based on this. But the responsibility to improve performance and customer satisfaction has been replaced with a responsibility to meet 95% of trains leaving on time. So all local decision making will be based on this and not on customer satisfaction. Can the regional manager trust each area manager or not? If the relationship is based on statistics alone then there is no relationship outside of the statistics.

People are clever - they will take advantage of statistics and work the system. Some examples I have come across are

> *Overall Objective:* Customer Satisfaction
> *Local Objective:* Phones must be answered within 3 rings
> *Outcome:*
> When you divert the phone the system does not count the rings, so everyone diverts the phone when they want a break, they achieve 100% but do not achieve customer satisfaction.
>
> *Overall Objective:* Resolve Problems Quickly
> *Local Objective:* Photocopying company told engineers they should not spend more than 20 minutes on a customer's site fixing photocopiers.
> *Outcome:*
> The engineers made sure the photocopier was working within 20 minutes but did not fix the core problem, they were visiting the same customer every week but were unwilling to spend the hour required to get the machine working properly.
>
> *Overall Objective:* Enhance Learning Experience
> *Local Objective:* Remember the HMI school earlier. The school was targeted with getting 95% of pupils to go on work experience but the school only had an 80% attendance record.
> *Outcome:*
> That school met its target! It sent letters to all the pupils informing them of their placement, then those that did not attend school that week were assumed to be on placement.
>> This actually had no benefit to anyone seeking a better education system.

Beware or the statistics required will drive the objectives rather than the objectives driving the statistics that are required. People will see the statistics as the end goal rather than the means to the end. If you do not allow for common sense, taking responsibility and local decision making then do not expect it – your train will leave empty but on time.

Φ Building Relationships

Leading on from the Statistics we need to build relationships. If we want success we cannot rely on measuring everything. We need to assess what level we need for each customer, colleague or partner. It will vary. As a (very, very) general guide it should be in direct proportion to the newness / uniqueness of the task for those involved and responsible. A builder's relationship with a supplier can be over the phone, he knows what to ask for and what to expect. But if I want to order bricks from the same supplier I need to be more involved, I need to know delivery methods, payments etc. I need to see the bricks because I do not know what the specifications mean….

We have to THINK and engage. Some questions to ask yourself when considering and assessing how you engage and relate and how much you need to invest in the engagement are:-

Are we asking for something that has not been done before?

Scratch below the surface – some people want you to think it is easy for them but we end up saying "this was not what I expected" – there can be misunderstandings or confusion later on, often after it is too late

Are we asking someone to do something they have not done before?

Am I responsible for these people or do they provide a service or product to my business?

What has been the results of previous engagements?

Remember we are building relationships to enable us to deliver, it will not be formulaic and there will be many different factors affecting how we work with other people.

Success versus Completion – Your Choice

Success and Failure   Page 80

Exercise – Carried Forward …

There is no exercise here. It is combined with a later section (see Page 96)

Φ Recap:
- Success and Failure
- Process Monkey
- Statistics
- Building Relationships

> Well done. Mrs Smith would like to invite us to her cat's "Welcome Home" party.

Success versus Completion – Your Choice

Templates and Guides

- JoeLee Nut – Tasty nut, some people addicted to it, some people allergic to it. Should really be taken in moderation and in relation to the quantity of other nuts in the bag

This section is a little bit different to the others. It is more technical and probably more tedious!

What I want to do is outline some good practices and techniques for managing a piece of work. I am not trying to make you an expert and I recommend that if you have a complex project you seriously consider both engaging an experienced Project Manager and using a recognised Project Management Method (there are many).

Success versus Completion – Your Choice

The following combination is very potent

- *Experienced Project Manager with ...*
- *...Experience of a Project Management method who ...*
- *...Understands the strengths and weaknesses of the method*

If your project is not so complicated as to need this then I highly recommend at least the following

- **Know Your Stakeholders**
- **Have a Plan**
- **Capture (and Publish) relevant Decisions and Minutes**
- **Manage Risks and Issues**

I would also encourage you to seriously consider the following

- **Milestones and Quality Gates**
- **Change Control**

Let's look at each in more detail but do not forget to read the rest of the book!

Φ Know Your Stakeholders

Stakeholders are anyone who is involved, not just those in authority, leaders or decision makers but also team members, interested parties, end users, staff, colleagues, contractors, customers, suppliers, etc. etc.

Most of us do this subconsciously in our daily lives. We know who is doing what activity, who is in charge, who we can get support from, who can make executive decisions....On a project it is important that everyone knows this so it might be worthwhile writing it down, but before doing this please re-visit the Pre-assignment section and use the exercise to write down your Project Objectives and Vision – why you are doing it and what you want to achieve. Use this as a precursor to any Stakeholder engagement so that all stakeholders are engaged and understand why they are involved.

For each Stakeholder it is worth capturing the following information but use your common sense, circumstances and project to decide what is best and how much detail in each

- Stakeholder Name
- Group – does this Stakeholder fit into a group of similar Stakeholders
- Type – Sponsor or Team Member or Customer or...
- Interest in project – High, Medium or Low usually works
- Influence over Project – High, Medium or Low
- How engaged are they – High, Medium or Low
- How are they Communicated with
  Weekly / Monthly / Never!
  Face to face / Phone / email

Add more entries as appropriate and keep it up to date.

Φ Have a Plan

This is essential. If you do not know where you are going the chances are you will end up lost!

1. Keep it Simple...
...but also with enough detail to keep track

Having a 3 week task called "Supply Telecomms Services" is all right if all you need to do is order from the supplier and then wait for them, but if you are the supplier then this is not good enough, you will need to break it down into various stages e.g.

Validate Order
Arrange Site Visit
Order Equipment
Install Cabling
Install Termination Equipment
Test line
Obtain Customer Sign Off

Success versus Completion – Your Choice

2. Treat it as a Tool…

…that enables you to achieve your goal. This essentially means two things

- Refer to it regularly and use it to keep track of progress
- Do not change it indiscriminately but be flexible – any changes should be assessed for their impact

3. You cannot plan in detail for a year in advance …

…So plan in stages

Plan the overall work at a high level but make sure you are reasonably confident of your timescales. For example have four 3 month sections with only 6-8 high level items per stage, half way through each stage there should be an activity to plan the next stage in more detail and to assess the overall plan.

4. Template

At the end of this section there is a template plan. Use it with caution. It will not do a lot for you unless **you** understand it and **you** can explain it to others.

Φ Capture and Publish Relevant Decisions and Minutes

This is also essential (although it can be tedious). Make sure decisions and actions are minuted and make sure you follow them through or follow them up. Use whatever seems best (spreadsheet, email, database, secretary …).

Φ Manage Risks and Issues

Identify what are your important Risks and Issues

- Risks are things that might happen
- Issues are things that have happened and need action

Keep them simple and reasonable, do not put in earthquakes or fatalities unless you are in an earthquake or war zone.

Templates and Guides

The Risks and Issues should be acted upon and have contingency activities (within reason), there is no point in capturing these unless you use it to your advantage.

There is a template at the end of the section. There are generally 4 things you can do with Risks – Eliminate, Transfer, Reduce or Accept. Although a lot if the time we actually do a combination of these.

Φ Milestones and Quality Gates

Milestones are key events in the plan. They can be anything but are usually

- A significant event (e.g. end of a stage)
- A significant delivery
- A high level event for senior management

Use them if you think they are beneficial

Quality Gates are used to pass from one stage to another. They usually consist of a checklist that needs to be agreed before moving on. They will require time, effort and commitment from all parties. Sometimes you need to add activities to your plan to assess, review and act at a Quality Gate

The following is a template / checklist for a Quality Gate but it will need to be adapted to the context and use.

- Description of Activity
- Date due for Completion
- Presenter / Presented By
- Key Stakeholders (i.e. those needed for sign off)
- Relevant Assumptions
- Relevant Decisions
- Relevant Risks
- Relevant Issues
- Relevant Actions
- Status of the Delivery
- Outcome (usually one of)
    Accepted
    Accepted with conditions

Success versus Completion – Your Choice

Rejected with conditions for re-submission
Rejected with reason

Φ Change Control

This involves tracking changes. This is required to inform all relevant stakeholders and get approval of any significant change. This could (and should) include changes to timescales.

Templates and Guides Page 87

Φ Templates Plan

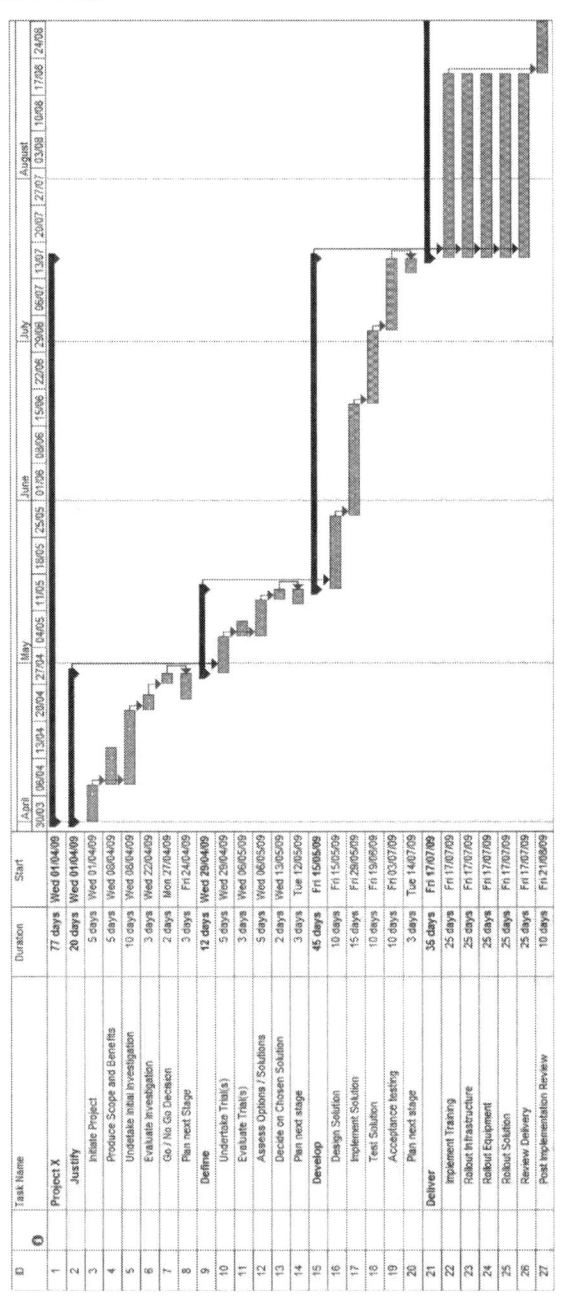

ID	Task Name	Duration	Start
1	Project X	77 days	Wed 01/04/09
2	Justify	20 days	Wed 01/04/09
3	Initiate Project	5 days	Wed 01/04/09
4	Produce Scope and Benefits	5 days	Wed 08/04/09
5	Undertake initial Investigation	10 days	Wed 08/04/09
6	Evaluate Investigation	3 days	Wed 22/04/09
7	Go / No Go Decision	2 days	Mon 27/04/09
8	Plan next Stage	3 days	Fri 24/04/09
9	Define	12 days	Wed 29/04/09
10	Undertake Trial(s)	5 days	Wed 29/04/09
11	Evaluate Trial(s)	3 days	Wed 06/05/09
12	Assess Options / Solutions	5 days	Wed 06/05/09
13	Decide on Chosen Solution	2 days	Wed 13/05/09
14	Plan next stage	3 days	Tue 12/05/09
15	Develop	45 days	Fri 15/05/09
16	Design Solution	10 days	Fri 15/05/09
17	Implement Solution	15 days	Fri 29/05/09
18	Test Solution	10 days	Fri 19/06/09
19	Acceptance testing	10 days	Fri 03/07/09
20	Plan next stage	3 days	Tue 14/07/09
21	Deliver	35 days	Fri 17/07/09
22	Implement Training	25 days	Fri 17/07/09
23	Rollout Infrastructure	25 days	Fri 17/07/09
24	Rollout Equipment	25 days	Fri 17/07/09
25	Rollout Solution	25 days	Fri 17/07/09
26	Review Delivery	25 days	Fri 17/07/09
27	Post Implementation Review	10 days	Fri 21/08/09

Success versus Completion – Your Choice

Templates and Guides

Φ Template Decisions and Minutes

An email / text template is as follows

ActNo	Owner	Progress
1/1	JC	**Complete.** Update plan with new delivery schedule
1/2	JC	**Ongoing.** Contact supplier x for …
2/1	JC	**New.** Ensure….

A spreadsheet example is as follows

Actions Project: Last updated: 14-May Last updated: 14-May

ACTION	DATE RAISED	DUE DATE	NEXT REVIEW	RAISED BY	OWNER	DESCRIPTION	UPDATE	STATUS	H/M/L
1/1	30/04/2009	14/05/2009	14/05/2009	John Coyle	John Coyle	Update plan with new	Completed 14/5	Closed	M
1/2	30/04/2009	31/05/2009	22/05/2009	John Coyle	John Coyle	Contact supplier x for …	Discussed with supplier. Expecting	Open	M
2/1	07/05/2009	30/06/2009	31/05/2009	John Coyle	John Coyle	Ensure…		Open	M
2/2									

Success versus Completion – Your Choice

Φ Template Risks

Risks

Project: Last updated: 14-May

Risk	Date Raised	Next Review Date	Raised by	Risk Description, inc. cause, impact and assumptions	Management/ Contingency Action	Person Responsible	Due Date	Impact 1 = Low 2 = Medium 3 = High	Probability 1 = Low 2 = Medium 3 = High	Weighted risk factor (Impact x Probability)	Status	Actual Closure Date	# Days Overdue
1	30-Apr-09	31-May-09	John Coyle	May have an external audit in June	Awaiting confirmation (or otherwise). If chosen will need to undertake an impact analysis	John Coyle	30-Jun	2	1	2	Open		0
2													
3													
4													
5													
6													
7													
8													
9													
10													

Success versus Completion – Your Choice

Templates and Guides

Φ Template Issues

Project:
Last updated: 14-May

Issues

Issue	Date Raised	Next Review Date	Raised by	Internal / External (I/E)	Issue Description, inc. cause, impact and assumptions	Action/ Mitigation With Named Action Owners	Person Responsible	Due Date	Impact 1 = Low 2 = Medium 3 = High	Urgency 1 = Low 2 = Medium 3 = High	Status Open Closed	Actual Closure Date	# Days Overdue
1	30-Apr-09	31-May-09	John Coyle	Internal	No Project Management experience in the team	Arranging training for team. Expecting confirmation by end of May	John Coyle	30-Jun-09	3	2	Open		0
2													
3													
4													
5													
6													
7													
8													
9													
10													

Success versus Completion – Your Choice

Section 4
Conclusion and Wrap Up

Success versus Completion – Your Choice

Review

What have we learnt?

Key Principles

- *1* - Identify your VALUES
- *2* - THINK
- *3* - Get a BALANCE
- *4* – Know Your SKILLS
- *5* – GROW (we can improve)

Application

- Pre-assignment
- Start up / Initiation / Arrival at a New Job, Project or Assignment
- Initiation to Stability (the first few weeks or months)
- Stability and Building on it
- Finishing, Signing Off and Getting Out
- Success and Failure throughout the cycle

… and Finally

Success versus Completion – Your Choice

Φ Conclusion

"I am forever in pursuit, but I don't even know what I am chasing. I've laboured for this moment for years like a madman - I raise my eyes and look down that corridor, 4 feet wide and 10 lonely seconds, to justify my whole existence - but will I? I've known fear of losing. I am now almost too frightened to win..."

Harold Abrahams
(Chariots of Fire, 100 yards winner
Paris 1920 Olympics)

Most of us do not define our lives (or even 4 years) in a day, let alone 10 seconds. We have neither the horror of failure nor the luxury of single mindedness - but our responsibilities bring their own horror and luxury. We have Defining Moments like the F1 example used earlier or the failure of the man during a power cut on Western Seaboard of the USA who stood for hours on a busy junction directing traffic and then on his way home was caught looting. These Defining Moments are not all or nothing but they go a long way to establishing our capabilities and character.

We also have Defining Characteristics, ideals that we aspire to like integrity or reliability. Mother Teresa of Calcutta said "We are not called to do extraordinary things. We are called to do the ordinary things extraordinarily well". These also go a long way to establishing our capabilities and character.

We can make a difference even if it is only small. Please do not give up on your values or vision but do not be fanatical either, get a **BALANCE**. I like the following story….

One evening on the coast there was a terrible storm, the sea washed over the promenade all night but by the morning everything was calm. A man went out for a walk on the beach, it was covered with jellyfish washed in by the storm and they were dying due to lack of water. He came across a small boy who was throwing the jellyfish back into the water. The man stopped the boy and pointed out all the jellyfish and said he could not hope to make a difference as hundreds if not thousands would die. The boy looked at the man, thought for a moment and then picked up another jellyfish and threw it in the water, he turned to the man and said "Well that sure made a difference to that jellyfish"

THINK also what will appear on your tombstone, who or what do you aspire to be? Do you want fame, fortune and achievements and have the following tombstone?

> Joe Bloggs
> Born dd/mmm/yyyy
> (with nothing)
> Died dd/mmm/yyyy
> (with x billion pounds/fans/power)
>
> Not missed – actually we would have liked to have got hold of his x billions earlier

Or do you aspire for things that you value and would you prefer the following tombstone

> Joe Bloggs
> Born dd/mmm/yyyy
> Died dd/mmm/yyyy
>
> Much missed family member, friend and colleague

Remember we are not trying to discover something new …

"This above all; to thine own self be true, it must follow, as the night follows day, thou canst not then be false to any man"
Polonius' advice to his son in Hamlet
William Shakespeare (1564-1616)

THINK. Do we want to be blown about by circumstances and moods (ours and others), by fashions and trends or will we have established a stability that enables us to steer (a reasonably) straight course? The analogy of steering or captaining a yacht is a good example. We have to deal with the conditions both good and bad, we have to use the skills and resources available to us and we have to get the yacht where we want it to go.

Success versus Completion – Your Choice

Have we worked out our Key Principles and are we continuing to work them out? Have we built up experience in applying them that enable us to understand better our way ahead? Do we step "Outside the Nutshell" often enough to gauge our perspective?

Not every captain will steer the yacht the exact same way or take the exact same route, it will not go in a straight line but will have to tack backwards and forwards all the time, and there will be setbacks - but if the captain is competent they will get there in reasonable time irrespective of the conditions - although the conditions will affect the timescale.

EXERCISE – CONCLUSION

There is a section at the end under Personal Focus for you to draw your Conclusions as well as to review Success and Failure (from the earlier chapter). Please take some time to review and complete (see Page 130)

"If"

If you can keep your head when all about you
Are losing theirs and blaming it on you;
If you can trust yourself when all men doubt you,
But make allowance for their doubting too;
If you can wait and not be tired by waiting,
Or being lied about, don't deal in lies,
Or being hated, don't give way to hating,
And yet don't look too good, nor talk too wise: . . .
(You will be a man my son)

If you can dream - and not make dreams your master;
If you can think - and not make thoughts your aim,
If you can meet with Triumph and Disaster
And treat those two impostors just the same;
If you can bear to hear the truth you've spoken
Twisted by knaves to make a trap for fools,
Or watch the things you've given your life to, broken,
And stoop and build 'em up with worn-out tools.

If you can make one heap of all your winnings
And risk it on one turn of pitch-and-toss,
And lose, and start again at your beginnings
And never breathe a word about your loss;
If you can force your heart and nerve and sinew
To serve your turn long after they are gone,
And so hold on when there is nothing in you
Except the Will which says to them: "Hold on."

If you can talk with crowds and keep your virtue,
Or walk with Kings - nor lose the common touch,
If neither foes nor loving friends can hurt you,
If all men count with you, but none too much;
If you can fill the unforgiving minute
With sixty seconds' worth of distance run,
Yours is the Earth and everything that's in it,
And - which is more - you'll be a Man, my son!

Rudyard Kipling (1865 – 1936)

Success versus Completion – Your Choice

SECTION 5
PERSONAL
FOCUS/EXERCISES

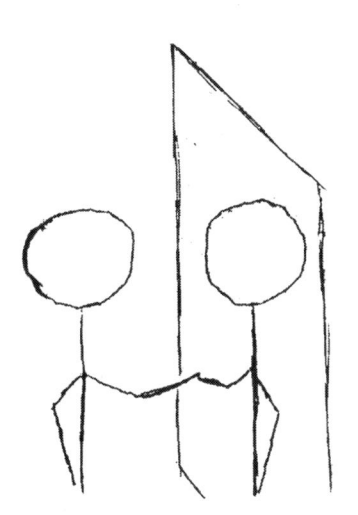

Success versus Completion – Your Choice

Success versus Completion – Your Choice

Personal Focus   Page 101

Φ *Exercise Introduction*

Please ensure you read this section at least once before you tackle any exercise.

As stated at the start of this book - you can use this book in any way that you want! Some suggested options were:-

- To read it
- To use it as part of a Development Programme with your colleagues / associates
- To read it and complete the exercises
- To carry it with you for reference

If you do decide to complete the exercises I would encourage you to do the following.

> *Take time over each exercise, think, assess, step back and re-visit. There are no better or best answers, it is what benefits you and your circumstances that matters.*

If you do decide to do the exercises you can do them individually or with a group.

Please feel free to read the whole book before tackling the exercises but please also tackle each exercise separately, read the relevant section of the book and take time over it.

The exercises will seem quite repetitive if you try to do them one after the other. The point is to focus on each subject, read the chapter and reflect on your own experiences.

There are exercises under the following subjects and each exercise refers back to the relevant section in the book:-

- Values
- Skills
- Objectives

Success versus Completion – Your Choice

- Start-Up
- Initiation to Stability
- Stability and Building on it
- Finishing
- Success, Failure and Conclusion

When doing the exercises please remember that each project, assignment or work package is different (sometimes considerably!). So, by all means, identify the problems of your last assignment but please do not try to fix them on your next assignment without asking yourself if it is important to do so or if there is a problem in the first place.

One of the things you will need to bear in mind is the Applied THINKing principle "take what you have learned previously and apply it to a new situation". Do not follow the same process time after time because it worked once. What you want to understand is why it worked and what it teaches you for the next time.

I will not repeat the above for every exercise but please bear it in mind.

Success versus Completion – Your Choice

Φ *Values*

Read the chapter on Values (see Page 17).

By reflecting on this and on what you understand to be important to you please take some time and write down your Values below.

This may take some time and your first attempt might instigate you to re-think and start again.

It may also be something that you want to re-visit regularly to hone and refine.

Please make sure you have read the Exercises Introduction (page 101) at least once before tackling any exercise.

What are your Values?

Personal Focus   Page 105

As we gain experience and learn and grow these may change so please feel free to re-visit and revise

Success versus Completion – Your Choice

Personal Focus

Φ *Skills*

Read the chapter on Identify your Skills (see Page 27).

Take some time and write down the Skills available to you below in the following pages.

First identify your Skills – this is what you think you are good at.

Then, on the second page, try to identify the Skills that are available to you.

Finally think how, in your current situation, you can best utilise these sets of skills.

In theory, your answers in the first part (your skills) are not going to change drastically over short periods of time, although your skills will change and improve over time.

The second and third part may change significantly as the people and resources around you change and as the job you have to do or deliver changes. Consequently it is worth revisiting these more regularly and at least every time you start a new assignment.

Please make sure you have read the Exercises Introduction (page 101) at least once before tacking any exercise.

VALUES + Applied THINKING + BALANCE + SKILLS => GROWTH

1) What are your Skills, Talents and Abilities?

Success versus Completion – Your Choice

2) What are the Skills, Talents and Abilities available to you?

Personal Focus

3) How can you best utilise the above sets of skills (yours <u>and</u> those available to you)?

_____
_____
_____
_____
_____
_____
_____
_____
_____
_____
_____
_____
_____
_____
_____
_____
_____
_____
_____
_____
_____
_____

As stated before as we gain experience and learn and grow these may change so please feel free to re-visit and revise.

Success versus Completion – Your Choice

Φ _Objectives_

Read the chapter on Pre-Assignment (see Page 37).

Take some time and write down your Objectives on the following pages.

These may be your current business Objectives but they may also be longer term and more achievement focused (either or both are fine).

If you do not know what your Objectives are then that may be your first entry - "Find out my Objectives".

If you are unsure then it may be possible to write down what you think they are and then bring in someone to review and give you feedback on them.

Objectives do not have to be long and complicated. The shorter and simpler the better.

I believe this can be looked at in two different ways.

1. Measurable Objectives

The first and the most commonly used are the performance related objectives, these are objectives we are expecting to review at the end of the period, give feedback on, decide how well they were achieved and possibly be used as input to a reward scheme. If you are doing this a good guideline is to ask if they are SMART

> **S** - Specific (i.e. not vague or unclear)
> **M** - Measurable
> **A** - Achievable
> **R** - Relevant (to the task in hand)
> **T** - Time Bound (is there a point in time that it should be done)

The chapter in the book explains some of the pros and cons around these.

2. Visionary Objectives

The second type are Visionary Objectives. This is the "step back and dream" type. These are often overlooked because they are very hard to measure. They can also overlap with your Ideals or Values – but this is OK.

I believe we should all have some Visionary Objectives but possibly they should be set by ourselves and measured informally. If someone does not want or does not agree with a Visionary Objective then we should probably not pursue it.

For example imagine someone who is good at putting forward their perspective and usually gives good input but is a bit too forthright.

> If they agree about being too forthright then we can say you need to be a bit more diplomatic and not speak out first at every meeting. This is hard to quantify but can be identified and supported.

> If they do not agree about being too forthright then all they may do is say nothing any more and achieve the objective but we will lose their valued input.

I would encourage you to write down your Measurable and your Visionary Objectives. As previously mentioned it is worth discussing with someone else so we can be more objective!

Please make sure you have read the Exercises Introduction (page 101) at least once before tackling any exercise.

1) What are your current Measurable Objectives?

Success versus Completion – Your Choice

2) What are your Visionary Objectives?

As stated before as we gain experience and learn and grow these may change so please feel free to re-visit and revise.

Success versus Completion – Your Choice

◊ *Start-Up*

Read the chapter on Start-Up (see Page 45).

At Start-Up we need to feel comfortable that we have the basics to enable us to progress. If the basics are not in place or people cannot answer our essential questions then we should be questioning the validity of the work or assignment.

Take some time and write down a maximum of 2 items in the following 3 topics.

Please make sure you have read the Exercises Introduction (page 101) at least once before tackling any exercise.

At Start-Up I have done the following well ...

_____
_____
_____
_____
_____
_____
_____
_____
_____
_____
_____

Personal Focus   Page 115

At Start-Up I should have done the following or done them better …

_____
_____
_____
_____
_____
_____
_____
_____
_____
_____

At Start-Up I should not have done the following …

_____
_____
_____
_____
_____
_____
_____
_____
_____
_____

Success versus Completion – Your Choice

Personal Focus

Reflect on the responses you have just made and write down a maximum of 4 items in each of the following 2 topics.

At Start-Up the following are Essential ...

Personal Focus

At Start-Up, from my experience, the following are Improvements that can be made ...

_____
_____
_____
_____
_____
_____
_____
_____
_____
_____
_____
_____
_____
_____
_____
_____
_____
_____
_____
_____
_____
_____

As stated before as we gain experience and learn and grow these may change so please feel free to re-visit and revise.

Success versus Completion – Your Choice

Personal Focus

Φ *Initiation to Stability*

Read the chapter on Initiation to Stability (see Page 55).

In the Initiation to Stability phase you are trying to ensure you do not let go of any of the essentials established in the Start-Up

Take some time and write down a maximum of 2 items in the following 3 boxes.

Please make sure you have read the Exercises Introduction (page 101) at least once before tackling any exercise.

During Initiation to Stability I have done the following well ...

_____
_____
_____
_____
_____
_____
_____
_____
_____
_____
_____
_____
_____

Success versus Completion – Your Choice

Personal Focus

During Initiation to Stability I should have done the following or done them better …

_____
_____
_____
_____
_____
_____
_____
_____
_____
_____

During Initiation to Stability I should not have done the following …

_____
_____
_____
_____
_____
_____
_____
_____
_____
_____

Success versus Completion – Your Choice

Reflect on the responses you have just made and write down a maximum of 4 items in each of the following 2 topics.

During Initiation to Stability the following are Essential ...

Personal Focus

During Initiation to Stability, from my experience, the following are Improvements that can be made …

_____

_____

_____

_____

_____

_____

_____

_____

_____

_____

_____

_____

_____

_____

_____

_____

_____

_____

_____

_____

As stated before as we gain experience and learn and grow these may change so please feel free to re-visit and revise.

Success versus Completion – Your Choice

Personal Focus

Φ *<u>Stability and Building on it</u>*

Read the chapter on Stability and Building on it (see Page 63).

During Stability you are trying to remember and remind people of what the essentials or the vision is and not to get caught up in just following a process with little understanding of why.

Take some time and write down a maximum of 2 items in the following 3 boxes.

Please make sure you have read the Exercises Introduction (page 101) at least once before tackling any exercise.

During Stability I have done the following well ...

_____
_____
_____
_____
_____
_____
_____
_____
_____
_____
_____

Personal Focus

During Stability I should have done the following or done them better …

___

During Stability I should not have done the following …

___

Success versus Completion – Your Choice

Personal Focus

Reflect on the responses you have just made and write down a maximum of 4 items in each of the following 2 topics.

During Stability the following are Essential ...

_____
_____
_____
_____
_____
_____
_____
_____
_____
_____
_____
_____
_____
_____
_____
_____
_____
_____
_____
_____
_____
_____
_____

Success versus Completion – Your Choice

Personal Focus

During Stability, from my experience, the following are Improvements that can be made ...

_____

As stated before as we gain experience and learn and grow these may change so please feel free to re-visit and revise.

Success versus Completion – Your Choice

Φ *Finishing*

Read the chapter on Finishing (see Page 69).

Finishing is drawing a line under the work but it is also involves leaving a positive influence as it is the last thing you do on the work or assignment.

Take some time and write down a maximum of 2 items in the following 3 boxes.

Please make sure you have read the Exercises Introduction (page 101) at least once before tackling any exercise.

When Finishing I have done the following well ...

_____
_____
_____
_____
_____
_____
_____
_____
_____
_____
_____
_____
_____
_____

Success versus Completion – Your Choice

When Finishing I should have done the following or done them better ...

_____
_____
_____
_____
_____
_____
_____
_____
_____

When Finishing I should not have done the following ...

_____
_____
_____
_____
_____
_____
_____
_____
_____
_____
_____

Success versus Completion – Your Choice

Personal Focus

Page 128

Reflect on the responses you have just made and write down a maximum of 4 items in each of the following 2 topics.

When Finishing the following are Essential …

Success versus Completion – Your Choice

Personal Focus

When Finishing, from my experience, the following are Improvements that can be made ...

_____
_____
_____
_____
_____
_____
_____
_____
_____
_____
_____
_____
_____
_____
_____
_____
_____
_____
_____
_____
_____
_____

As stated before as we gain experience and learn and grow these may change so please feel free to re-visit and revise.

Success versus Completion – Your Choice

Personal Focus

Φ *Success, Failure and Conclusion*

Read the chapters on Success and Failure (see Page 73) and the Conclusion (see Page 91).

Take some time and write down what your key learning points are from reading this book.

It might be the most important learning from earlier exercises, it might be to review all or some of the exercises regularly or it might be something that is not in the book but which came to mind from reading the book.

I would suggest a maximum of three.

Please make sure you have read the Exercises Introduction (page 101) at least once before tackling any exercise.

Key Learning Point No. 1

_____
_____
_____
_____
_____
_____
_____
_____
_____
_____
_____

Success versus Completion – Your Choice

Key Learning Point No. 2

Key Learning Point No. 3

As stated before as we gain experience and learn and grow these may change so please feel free to re-visit and revise.

Success versus Completion – Your Choice

Φ *Notes*

Finally this section is for any further notes you may have…..

Notes

Notes

Notes

Notes

Notes

Success versus Completion – Your Choice

INDEX

Success versus Completion – Your Choice

Index

A
Abrahams, Harold, 94
Achievements, 66

B
Balance, 23, 24, 27, 29, 40, 41, 43, 49, 56, 68, 94

C
Celebrate, 66, 71
Change Control, 86
Competence, 66
Completion, 5, 6
Concernl, 39
Conclusion, 70, 91, 130
Correct Mistakes, 66
Covey, Stephen R., 38, 39, 52

D
De-brief, 71
Decisions, 84, 88
Delegation, 52
Detours, 58
Dick, Frank, 74
Dickens, Charles, 64

E
Edwards, Jonathan, 23
Exercise, 99

F
Failure, 71, 73, 130
Finishing, 69, 126

G
Grow, 40, 42, 64
Growth, 29, 30, 51
Guides, 81

H
Hammarskjold, Dag, 41

I
Implement, 70
Influence, 39
Initiation to Stability, 55, 118
Integrity, 40, 46
Issues, 82, 84, 90

J
John Paul II, 50

K
Kipling, Rudyard, 97

L
Lao Tzo, 67
Leadership, 67
Learn, 42
Lombardi, Vince, 56, 74

M
Milestones, 85
Minutes, 84, 88
Mistakes, 66
Mother Teresa, 94
Muhammad Ali, 42, 48, 74

N
Niebuhr, Reinhold, 39
Notes, 132
Nutshell, 4, 22, 42, 57, 96

O
Objectives, 38, 110

Orwell, George, 67

P

Partners, 59
Plan, 82, 83, 87
Pre-assignment, 37
Process Monkey, 75
Project Activities, 49
Project Management, 46
Pursuing Progress, 50

Q

Quality Gates, 82, 85

R

Relationships, 79
Remain Conscious, 42
Resources, 51
Risks, 82, 84, 89

S

Shakespeare, William, 95

Sign Off, 71
Skills, 27, 28, 29, 40, 66, 106
Stability and Building on it, 122
Stability and Building on it, 63
Stakeholders, 82
Start-Up, 45, 114
Statistics, 77
Success, 3, 5, 6, 38, 66, 71, 73, 130

T

Team Building, 64
Team Management, 53
Team Player, 65
Teamwork, 56
Templates, 81, 87
Think, 21, 22, 27, 29, 40, 43, 59, 70, 71, 76, 79, 95
Twain, Mark, 77

V

Values, 17, 19, 27, 29, 40, 104

About the Author

John Coyle is a seasoned professional project and programme manager. With over 20 years' experience, mainly but not exclusively in the Telecomms and IT world. He has delivered significant projects in both private and public sectors. He has worked for a small software house, for the public sector and for large multi-national corporations. He has experience as both the supplier/vendor and as the customer/end-user. He has delivered systems to control nuclear power stations, developed a Command and Control system for the Ambulance Service, managed a software vendor for a large corporation, and delivered telecommunication solutions and various transformation initiatives in large corporations.

John's varied experience of dealing with a wide variety of people in an equally wide range of situations and circumstances extends to roles outside his professional work, including, as an active member of his church, organising several large international conferences and events.

John is married to Mary and they have 5 sons.